822.914
R89t

144262

DATE DUE			

Tom

Twayn

Kinley E

Northeast

TOM STOPPARD, 1983
Photograph courtesy of
Dr. Miriam Stoppard

Tom Stoppard

By Susan Rusinko

Twayne Publishers • Boston

Tom Stoppard

Susan Rusinko

Copyright © 1986 by G.K. Hall & Co.
All Rights Reserved
Published by Twayne Publishers
A Division of G.K. Hall & Co.
70 Lincoln Street
Boston, Massachusetts 02111

First Paperback Edition, 1986

Copyediting supervised by Lewis DeSimone
Book production by Elizabeth Todesco
Book design by Barbara Anderson

Typeset in 11 pt. Garamond
by P&M Typesetting, Inc., Waterbury, Connecticut

Printed on permanent/durable acid-free paper
and bound in the United States of America

Library of Congress Cataloging in Publication Data

Rusinko, Susan
    Tom Stoppard.

    (Twayne's English authors series; TEAS 419)
    Bibliography: p. 152
    Includes index.
    1. Stoppard, Tom—Criticism and interpretation.
I. Title. II. Series.
PR6069.T6Z86   1986   822'.914   85-17589
ISBN 0-8057-6909-9
ISBN 0-8057-6927-7 (pbk.)

For Mary Rusinko, Anna Costa, John Rusinko, and Helen Schutz

Contents

TOM STOPPARD

About the Author

Author of *Terence Rattigan*, also in the Twayne English Authors Series, Susan Rusinko has contributed reviews and articles to *The Shaw Review*, *The Annual of Bernard Shaw Studies*, *Modern Drama*, *World Literature Today*, *Dictionary of Literary Biography*, and *Critical Surveys*. She wrote her doctoral thesis on Harold Pinter, and, as professor of English at Bloomsburg University of Pennsylvania, she teaches modern drama. Her theater interests take her on regular trips to New York and London and include teaching biennial theater study courses in London.

Preface

Tom Stoppard's high comedies of ideas, as he has labeled them, have earned for him a reputation as a witty dramatist unequaled in this genre since the advent of Shaw and Wilde at the turn of the century. The major difference between him and his famous predecessors lies in the purpose for which their wit is engaged. For Shaw, social reformer, there was an economic, political, and moral matrix that directed his brilliant debates. His thesis drama broke new ground, making him the towering figure of the English stage during the first half of the twentieth century. Similarly, Wilde, farcically satirizing contemporary mores, devastated conventional morality, writing comedies of manners more than of ideas.

In the tradition of Shaw and Wilde, Stoppard once again has made the stage a forum for ideas and a showcase for daringly inventive use of the language. Unlike them, however, he elaborately structures his debates in the course of the play, only to dismantle them by the end, sometimes quite suddenly. This process is one of the many ambushes Stoppard lays for his unsuspecting audiences. He insists that he does not take sides in the debates, fearing, perhaps, like one of his characters, that he would lose himself in them if he did. His process of continuous contradiction, brilliantly realized, has garnered high critical praise. Yet there are voices, although in the minority, such as Robert Brustein and Martin Gottfried, who are skeptical of what Stoppard does with his ideas. And in this respect, Stoppard remains apart from both Shaw and Wilde whose wit was purposeful and whose ideas, particularly Shaw's, were carefully and elaborately explored.

Of *Rosencrantz and Guildenstern Are Dead*, Brustein writes that Stoppard manipulates "the premise instead of exploring it and what results is merely an immensely shrewd exercise enlivened more by cunning than by conviction."[1] Of the same drama, Gottfried writes that a philosophical statement is hammered at but "never developed beyond the basic statement. Its existentialism is shallow."[2] And Irving Wardle speaks of Stoppard's later play, *The Real Thing*, as "cleverness with its back to the wall."[3]

More important, perhaps, than intellectual gymnastics performed with ideas are the gymnastics of his language. Again, he has an illustrious predecessor, James Joyce, who created a new langauge for the novel of the twentieth century. Stoppard, without creating a new langauge, but seeming to do so by the dazzling use to which he puts existing language, has had a similar effect on the stage. This is particularly well illustrated in *Travesties,* which is a total indulgence in and intoxication with linguistic rhythms and images. Indeed, Joyce is a character in this play, and his style is richly parodied by Stoppard.

Yet a third characteristic, as theatrical as his manipulation of ideas and language, is Stoppard's creative plagiarizing of other writers, a plagiarism that provides him with a peg on which to hang his plots. Borrowing from Shakespeare, Beckett, Sophocles, Christie, Wilde, Miller, and others, he has reinvented their characters and situations for his own time and vision.

Indeed, whole scenes from *Hamlet, Macbeth, The Importance of Being Earnest, Miss Julie,* and *'Tis a Pity She's a Whore* are built into his plays. Long passages from Eliot's "The Love Song of J. Alfred Prufrock" appear in his novel, *Lord Malquist and Mr. Moon.* In his play about journalists, *Night and Day,* the influence of Waugh's novel *Scoop* is strong.

His slightly hostile views of critics and academics notwithstanding, Stoppard himself was once a critic, and he has relied on his reading of academics for some of his subjects. Richard Ellmann's study of Joyce, G. E. Moore's philosophical writings, Lenin's treatises, and Edmund Wilson's *The Wound and the Bow* are acknowledged sources. In fact, to enjoy Stoppard's dramatic jokes and his audience ambushes requires a literary literacy that only the sophisticated theatergoer possesses. What Stoppard may have most in common with Shaw, Joyce, Eliot, and Beckett is the pleasure of an audience that consciously or unconsciously identifies a familiar allusion in its fresh context.

The dazzling displays of ideas, language, and inventive parodic style of Stoppard's dramas have drawn criticism, almost from the start, about the absence of social or political conscience in those dramas. He silenced that criticism in the late 1970s when, along with his own personal activism in campaigns for human rights in Eastern Europe, he wrote a series of political plays: *Professional Foul, Every Good Boy Deserves Favour,* and *Dogg's Hamlet, Cahoot's Mabeth.*

Preface

Still another criticism has haunted Stoppard's writing: his inability to develop a character emotionally. He responded to this charge in a comment to Kenneth Tynan: "But you ask me about expressing emotion. Let me put the best possible light on my inhibitions and say that I'm waiting until I can do it well."[4] And of Derek Marlow's charge that he couldn't understand women, Stoppard said that he would have understood it if Marlowe had said *people* rather than *women*.[5] Both of these criticisms, however, have been triumphantly silenced in Stoppard's play about marital infidelities, *The Real Thing*. Joining the symphony of rave reviews of the New York production, Frank Rich has described it as not only the "most moving play but also the most bracing play that anyone has written about love and marriage in years."[6] Into this play, "so densely and entertainingly packed with wit, ideas and feelings that one visit just won't do,"[7] Stoppard has poured the inventiveness of his earlier comedies of ideas and the emotional intensity lacking in the earlier plays. Like the main character, a dramatist named Henry, Stoppard has indeed learned to "write love."

Like Shaw, Stoppard began his career on the stage as a theater critic, and like Shaw and Wilde, he has provided audiences with refreshingly articulate characters whose language has invigorated the modern stage.

In this study of Stoppard's work, each of his full-length stage dramas (including *Enter a Free Man*, originally a television play) and his novel are treated in individual chapters, with the remaining short or lesser stage plays, radio and television dramas, screenplays, and stage adaptations discussed in chapters devoted to the respective genres. Within this arrangement, the Stoppardian hero is traced from the Boot and Moon characters of *Lord Malquist and Mr. Moon* to their incarnations in later plays. The new hero, as defined by Stoppard's dramas, succeeds if he creates and controls his own context, or fails if he disappears into the existing context.

Susan Rusinko

Bloomsburg University of Pennsylvania

Acknowledgments

I wish to thank Virginia Duck for her many hours of proofreading, Joan Walton for arranging typing assistance in the preparation of this manuscript, and Sandra Smith for locating sources in library indexes. The following permissions to quote are acknowledged:

Reprinted by permission of Faber and Faber Ltd., London: *Introduction 2: Stories by New Writers* © 1964 by Tom Stoppard; *Undiscovered Country* © 1980 by Tom Stoppard; *On the Razzle* © 1981 by Tom Stoppard; *The Real Thing* © 1982 by Tom Stoppard.

Reprinted by permission of Grove Press, Inc., New York and Faber and Faber Ltd., London: *Enter a Free Man* © 1968 by Tom Stoppard; *Every Good Boy Deserves Favour* and *Professional Foul* © 1972 by Tom Stoppard; *Jumpers* © 1972 by Tom Stoppard; *The Real Inspector Hound* © 1968 by Tom Stoppard; *Rosencrantz and Guildenstern Are Dead* © 1967 by Tom Stoppard; *Travesties* © 1975 by Tom Stoppard; *"Albert's Bridge" and Other Plays* © 1969 and 1973 by Tom Stoppard; *"Dirty Linen" and "New-Found-Land"* © 1976 by Tom Stoppard; *Night and Day* © 1979 by Tom Stoppard; *Lord Malquist and Mr. Moon* © 1966 by Tom Stoppard.

Chronology

1937   Born Tomas Straussler, 3 July, in Zlin (now Gottwaldov), Czechoslovakia, second son of Eugene and Martha Straussler.

1939   Family is moved to Singapore by Bata (now Svit), shoe manufacturer for whom father is company doctor.

1942   Family is evacuated to Darjeeling, India, on eve of Japanese invasion. Father, who remained behind, is killed. Sons attend multinational American school.

1946   Martha Straussler marries Kenneth Stoppard, British army major. Family moves to England.

1946–1954   Attends Dolphin School in Nottinghamshire and Pocklington School in Yorkshire. Family moves to Bristol.

1954–1958   After leaving school at 17, works for *Western Daily Press* and *Bristol Evening World*.

1960   H. M. Tennent options *A Walk on the Water*, Stoppard's first play.

1962–1963   Moves to London and reviews plays for *Scene* magazine, writing under pseudonym, William Boot.

1963   *A Walk on the Water*, ITV, November.

1964   *This Way Out with Samuel Boot*, ninety-minute TV play, unproduced. *The Dissolution of Dominic Boot*, BBC Radio, 20 February. *"M" Is for Moon Among Other Things*, BBC Radio, 6 April. Attends Ford Foundation drama colloquium in Berlin. Writes one-act verse play, *Rosencrantz and Guildenstern Meet King Lear*. Publishes three short stories in *Introduction 2: Stories by New Writers*.

1965   Marries Jose Ingle (who becomes the mother of their sons, Oliver and Barnaby). Writes episodes for *A Student's Diary*, BBC Radio. *A Walk on the Water*, BBC Radio, November.

1966   *If You're Glad I'll Be Frank*, BBC Radio, 8 February. Adaptation of Mrozek's *Tango*, RSC, Aldwych Theatre,

25 May. *A Separate Peace,* BBC TV, 22 August. *Rosencrantz and Guildenstern Are Dead,* Cranston Hall, Edinburgh, 24 August. *Lord Malquist and Mr. Moon* is published, August.

1967   *Teeth,* BBC TV, 7 February. *Rosencrantz and Guildenstern Are Dead,* Old Vic, 11 April. *Another Moon Called Earth,* BBC TV, 28 June. *Albert's Bridge,* BBC Radio, 13 July. *Rosencrantz and Guildenstern Are Dead,* Alvin Theater, New York, 16 October. Wins John Whiting award and *Evening Standard* award.

1968   *Enter A Free Man,* St. Martin's Theatre, 28 March. *The Real Inspector Hound,* Criterion Theatre, 17 June. *Neutral Ground,* Thames TV, 11 December. Wins Prix Italia for *Albert's Bridge;* Tony and New York Critics Circle awards for *Rosencrantz and Guildenstern Are Dead.*

1970   *Where Are They Now?,* BBC Radio, 28 January. *The Engagement,* NBC TV (U.S.), 8 March. *After Magritte,* Green Banana Restaurant, 9 April.

1972   Divorces Jose Ingle, 31 January. Marries Dr. Miriam Moore-Robinson (who becomes the mother of their sons, William and Edmund). *Jumpers,* Old Vic, 2 February, winner of *Evening Standard* and *Plays and Players* awards. *After Magritte* and *The Real Inspector Hound,* Theater Four, New York, 23 April; also at Shaw Theatre, 6 November. *Artist Descending a Staircase,* BBC Radio, 14, November.

1973   Adaptation of Lorca's *The House of Bernarda Alba,* Greenwich Theatre, 22 March.

1974   *Travesties,* Aldwych Theatre, 10 June. *Jumpers,* Billy Rose Theater, New York, 22 April.

1975   Screenplay of Thomas Wiseman's novel, *The Romantic Englishwoman, Dirty Linen* and *New-Found-Land,* Almost Free Theatre, 6 April. *Boundaries,* with Clive Exton, BBC TV series. *Travesties,* Ethel Barrymore Theater, New York, 30 October.

1976   *The (15 Minute) Dogg's Troupe Hamlet,* terraces of National Theatre, 24 August. Wins Tony award for *Travesties.*

1977   *Dirty Linen* and *New-Found-Land,* Golden Theater, New York, 11 January. *Every Good Boy Deserves Favour,* Royal Festival Hall, 1 July. *Professional Foul,* BBC TV, September, winner of British Television Critics award.

1978   *Professional Foul,* WNET TV (U.S.), April. *Night and Day,* Phoenix Theatre, 8 November, winner of *Evening Standard* award. Writes screenplay of Nabokov's novel *Le Meprise.* Awarded CBE.

1979   *Dogg's Hamlet, Cahoot's Macbeth,* Arts Centre, University of Warwick, 26 May; Collegiate Theatre, 30 July. Adaptation of Schnitzler's *Das Weite Land* as *Undiscovered Country,* Olivier Theatre, 20 June. *Dogg's Hamlet, Cahoot's Macbeth,* 22 Steps Theater, New York, 3 October. *Night and Day,* Anta Theater, New York, 27 November. *Every Good Boy Deserves Favour,* Metropolitan Opera, New York, 30 July. Writes screenplay for Greene's novel, *The Human Factor.*

1980   Receives honorary degrees from Universities of Leeds and Sussex.

1981   Writes screenplay for P. D. James's novel *Innocent Blood.* Adapts Nestroy's *Einen Jux Will Er Sich Machen* as *On the Razzle,* Lyttleton Theatre, 18 September. D. Litt., University of Warwick.

1982   *The Dog It Was That Died,* BBC Radio. Writes *Squaring the Circle* for television. *The Real Thing,* Strand Theatre, 17 November.

1984   *The Real Thing,* Plymouth Theater, New York, 5 January; Tony awards for best play, direction (Mike Nichols), leading actor and actress (Jeremy Irons and Glenn Close), and featured actress (Christine Baranski). *Squaring the Circle,* ITV, 31 May. Adaptation of Molnar's *Play at the Castle* as *Rough Crossing,* Lyttleton Theatre, 30 October.

Chapter One
A Bounced Czech

When questioned by interviewers and lecture audiences about influences, meanings, and ideas in his plays, over and over Tom Stoppard has insisted on the secondary importance of these matters. He is equally insistent on the primacy of theater as an event and of events in his plays that must work on stage. If they do not work, they are thrown out or altered. Meanings and ideas have their place as they develop from the theatrical events. No play or part of a play for Stoppard is sacrosanct as written and is always subject to changes dictated by its workability on stage.

As literary texts, his plays seem almost not to exist for this Czechoslovakian-born dramatist, whose own life is a pastiche of events that have taken him to Singapore, Darjeeling, and finally to England. The events that overtook Rosencrantz and Guildenstern and, indeed, so many characters in Stoppard's plays, take on a curiously biographical cast. For these two Shakespearean characters who attempt to understand why they are in Elsinore, little is certain. "A man standing in his saddle and in the half-lit half-alive dawn banged on the shutters and called two names. He was just a hat and a cloak levitating in the grey plume of his own breath, but when he called we came. That much is certain—we came."[1]

This minuscule certainty, the only still point in a universe of positive uncertainties, determines and pervades Stoppard's imaginative world. It was present in a literal way in his arriving in Edinburgh in August 1966 to rescue a production of *Rosencrantz and Guildenstern Are Dead,* in a Cranston Street church hall, from what seemed to the company like imminent disaster. He revised the last two acts to get rid of clogging repetitions and to settle some directing problems. That he came was certain; after that, events unrolled, and an important part of English stage history began to take shape.

The events of Stoppard's life reflect the leapfrogging events dramatized in his plays. Born 3 July 1937 in Zlin, Czechoslovakia, the younger of two sons, to Dr. and Mrs. Eugene Straussler, he was only two years old when, on the eve of Hitler's move into that country, his father, a company doctor at Bata, an international shoe company, was transferred to Singapore. Prior to the Japanese invasion of Singapore, his mother and her two sons were again moved, this time to India. In Darjeeling Stoppard's mother managed a Bata shoe shop, and the boys attended a multinational American school. Dr. Straussler was killed during the Japanese invasion, and Mrs. Straussler later married Major Kenneth Stoppard, who moved the family to England in 1946. Tom Stoppard's education continued at the Dolphin School in Nottinghamshire and at Pocklington School in Yorkshire. "Thoroughly bored by the idea of anything intellectual," gladly selling "all my Greek and Latin classics to George's Bookshop in Park Street" and "totally bored and alienated by everyone from Shakespeare to Dickens besides,"[2] he describes the chief influence of education as a negative one.

His stepfather, who was in the machine tool industry, moved the family from place to place, finally arriving in Bristol, where at seventeen Tom Stoppard joined the *Western Daily Press*. His journalistic writing consisted of news reporting, a lot of feature writing, and even an odd color piece. After four years there, he wrote for the *Evening World,* where his interest in the theater began. Moving to London and to *Scene,* a short-lived magazine, he wrote theater reviews. Within seven months on the staff he had reviewed 132 plays under the pseudonym of William Boot, a character from Waugh's novel *Scoop.* The name Boot recurs in a number of Stoppard's plays.

Meantime, Stoppard had published three short stories ("Life, Times: A Fragment," "Reunion," and "The Story") and written two radio plays (*"M" Is for Moon Among Other Things,* about Marilyn Monroe's death, and *The Dissolution of Dominic Boot*). An option on his play *A Walk on the Water* had been purchased by a commercial television company. These efforts he describes as the "transition to living off playwriting."[3]

About the time that *Scene* magazine folded, Stoppard was granted a Ford Foundation award to a Berlin colloquium for promising young playwrights. Between May and October 1964, he wrote a Shakespearean pastiche, *Rosencrantz and Guildenstern Meet King Lear.* Two years later the piece had grown into a full-length play, produced at the Edinburgh Festival. The next year on the stage of the National Theatre at the Old Vic, Stoppard's career as dramatist was convincingly launched with the play that still remains in the opinion of many critics his chief work, *Rosencrantz and Guildenstern Are Dead.* In addition to the auspicious Edinburgh debut of the play, 1966 is important as the release date of his only novel, *Lord Malquist and Mr. Moon,* commissioned by Anthony Blond. Having expected a favorable review, Stoppard was surprised when it was the play and not the novel that garnered positive notices.

In 1965 Stoppard married Jose Ingle, a nurse. Two sons, Oliver and Barnaby, were born of that marriage. Divorced in 1972, Stoppard married Dr. Miriam Moore-Robinson, a medical director of Syntex Pharmaceuticals and a television personality known for her articulateness in discussing medical issues for women. She is the author of two books on health hints for women. Two sons, William and Edmund, were born to Stoppard's second marriage. The four sons reside with the Stoppards in Iver Heath, just outside London.

Stoppard's writing in 1965 included seventy episodes of *A Student's Diary,* a serial about an Arab in London, translated into Arabic and broadcast on BBC Radio. In addition, *A Walk on the Water* and *If You're Glad I'll Be Frank* were broadcast on BBC Radio and *A Separate Peace* on BBC Television.

The awards began coming in. He received the John Whiting award (jointly with David Storey) from the Arts Council and the *Evening Standard* award as the most promising playwright in 1967. In America he won both the Tony award and the Drama Critics' Circle award for *Rosencrantz and Guildenstern Are Dead.* In addition, *Teeth* and *Another Moon Called Earth* were broadcast on BBC TV, and *Albert's Bridge* (BBC Radio) won the Prix Italia.

Play followed play—on stage, radio, and television—as *Enter A Free Man* (revised from *A Walk on the Water*) and *The Real Inspector Hound* opened on the London stage in 1968 and *After Magritte* in 1969. Additional short plays—*Where Are They Now?* and *The Engagement*—were aired on BBC Radio and Television respectively.

Stoppard's second major play, *Jumpers,* produced by the National Theatre at the Old Vic in 1972, received the *Evening Standard* award and the *Plays and Players* award as the best play of the year. *Jumpers* was followed two years later by *Travesties,* the third of the major dramas. Both productions enjoyed success in both London and New York, and Stoppard's reputation for dazzling images and linguistic pyrotechnics reached new heights. *"Dirty Linen" and "New-Found-Land,"* two plays in one, is Stoppard's tribute to America's bicentennial celebration in 1976.

Up to this time, Stoppard had rejected the notion of social commitment in his writing. Like Harold Pinter, he insisted on the primacy of theater as an event in and of itself and not as a forum for ideas or causes. Although ideas and political causes may grow from that event, they are neither the beginning nor the end of the play. More recently, however, political protests have appeared in his personal and professional life. As a member of the Committee Against Psychiatric Abuse in 1975, he spoke at a rally in Trafalgar Square and marched to the Soviet embassy to petition for the rights of Soviet citizens. In 1977 he visited Moscow, Leningrad, and Prague with an Amnesty International official. He wrote long newspaper articles and letters on behalf of political freedom. In Czechoslovakia he met dissident playwrights Vaclav Havel and Pavel Kohout.

That same year *Every Good Boy Deserves Favour* (about Eastern European political prisoners), with music composed by André Previn, was performed at the Royal Festival Hall in London and at the Metropolitan Opera House in New York. Also in 1977 *Professional Foul* (about English academicians at a Czechoslovakian philosophical congress) was aired in England and the next year in America.

Although not advocating any particular political cause, *Night and Day* (1978) is a play about newspapermen involved in an African revolution. It received attention as a naturalistic drama about various journalistic types rather than as political commentary. The generally mixed reviews emphasized Stoppard's seeming change of stylistic direction from the imaginatively innovative techniques of his earlier plays to a more naturalistic and, consequently, lesser mode. *The Real Thing* (1982) also opened to similar critical reception in London.

Scattered among his six full-length stage plays (three of which stand out sharply as his major work) and his many radio, television, and shorter stage plays are his stage adaptations: Lorca's *The House of Bernarda Alba*, Mrozek's *Tango*, Schnitzler's *Das Weite Land* (*Undiscovered Country*), and Nestroy's *Einen Jux Will Er Sich Machen* (*On the Razzle*). His screen adaptations include Wiseman's *The Romantic Englishwoman*, Nabokov's *Le Meprise*, Graham Greene's *The Human Factor*, P. D. James's *Innocent Blood*, and the television adaptation of Jerome K. Jerome's *Three Men in a Boat*.

Degrees have been conferred on Stoppard by Brunel University (1979), the Universities of Leeds and Sussex (1980), and the University of Warwick (1981). He is the recipient of the Shakespeare Prize of the FVS Foundation, Hamburg (1979), and of the C.B.E. (1978). All this recognition has come to a dramatist still in his forties. Like his two famous characters Rosencrantz and Guildenstern, whose certainty is that they came to Elsinore, so amongst the positive uncertainties of events—from Czechoslovakia, Singapore, and India to England—certainty of recognition has come to Stoppard.

Above all, Stoppard prefers the quiet of life in Iver Heath, a London suburb, where his family and his writing constitute his life.

Kenneth Tynan's description of Stoppard is as apropriate a conclusion as any for a biographical sketch of the dramatist:

[It is] essential to remember that Stoppard is an émigré. A director who has staged several of his plays told me the other day, "You have to be foreign to write English with that kind of hypnotized brilliance." . . . Stoppard loves all forms of wordplay, especially puns, and frequently describes himself as a "bounced Czech." . . . Nowadays, he is *plus anglais que les anglais*—a phrase that would please him, as a student of linguistic caprice, since it implies that his English can best be defined in French.[4]

Chapter Two
Stoppard and Pinter

When *Look Back in Anger* by John Osborne opened at the Royal Court Theatre in London in 1956, forces were unleashed on the stage to open up a new era in English dramatic history. What happened was hailed immediately by critics and theater-goers as the dawn of a new age. Its effect was felt on stages other than English, as the term "angry young men" took hold of the imagination of actors, directors, writers, and audiences.

The prevailing drama had run its course. Shaw, who had begun his own revolution with the highly articulate thesis drama more than fifty years earlier, had died. The experiments in poetic drama by writers such as T. S. Eliot and Christopher Fry did not result in the anticipated infusion of new life in the theater. And Noel Coward and Terence Rattigan, with their well-shaped, articulately upper-middle-class dramas, commanded the lion's share of popularity.

Then came Jimmy Porter, Osborne's hero, from whose anger the new age derived its label, the angry theater. Bursting on the stage, raw emotions exploding with fury at the dreariness, monotony, and bleak future of lower-middle-class life in the midlands and, ultimately, at the absence of great causes such as the Spanish Civil War during the 1930s, Porter released the pent-up frustration of a whole post–World War II generation.

Two dramatists, among the many affected by Osborne's drama, were Terence Rattigan and Tom Stoppard. Rattigan, then forty-five, England's establishment playwright, was enjoying the second spectacularly successful year of *Separate Tables,* two of whose main characters, a journalist and his estranged wife, bore subdued resemblance to Jimmy and Alison Porter in *Look Back in Anger*. After attending the opening at the Royal Court, Rattigan made his frequently repeated comment that playwrights would henceforth be measured by the reaction: "Look how unlike Terence Rattigan I'm being."[1]

If an established dramatist such as Rattigan felt the impact of Osborne's play, no less did the younger generation of playwrights, among whom was nineteen-year-old Tom Stoppard. "Like a lot of other people I started writing plays not very long after being moved to tears and laughter by *Look Back in Anger*."² "After *Look Back in Anger* young writers tended to be young playwrights, not because what they had to say I think was particularly suited to dramatic form but because the theatre was clearly the most interesting and dynamic medium."³ Stoppard's own interest in the stage had developed in his journalistic years as newsreporter, feature writer, theater critic, and gossip columnist.

Although Osborne's play structure and naturalistic poetry are hardly what one would call innovative, his conventional style was overshadowed by his subject matter: the violently honest emotions of an antihero expressed for the first time on the London stage. Twenty-five years later, Jimmy Porter, the character, is remembered more than is the play as a whole.

Indeed, the real stage revolution occurred soon after in the plays of two writers who challenged the existing stage language with their stylistic and linguistic innovations: Harold Pinter and Tom Stoppard. With Samuel Beckett as their acknowledged literary progenitor, Pinter and Stoppard assaulted conventional dramaturgy, Stoppard admitting his debt, as well, to Wilde, Joyce, Eliot, and, of course, Shakespeare. Seven years younger than Pinter, Stoppard became the major dramatist in what has been called the second wave of new dramatists during the 1970s, just as Pinter had led the first wave during the 1960s.

It was only one year after *Look Back in Anger* (1956) that Pinter's first play, *The Room* (1957), was produced, and ten years later that Stoppard's *Rosencrantz and Guildenstern Are Dead* was hailed at the Edinburgh Festival as a major new play.

Pinter and Stoppard share common backgrounds and interests. Both have recent origins in central-eastern Europe, Pinter's forebears having emigrated from Hungary at the turn of the century and Stoppard himself having arrived in England in 1946 at the age of nine. Pinter is Jewish, and Stoppard is partly Jewish. Neither Stoppard nor Pinter attended university, the former choosing to enter journalism and the latter, acting. Both were in their apprentice years when the Osborne revolution broke.

Other common interests of Pinter and Stoppard include a love of cricket, which they indulge annually in their match with a team from the *Guardian*. In his article for the *New Yorker*, later published in

Show People, Kenneth Tynan entertainingly recounts one of these annual fixtures.

Further personal similarities extend to their first marriages, both of which went stale with success. Stoppard has remarried, to a doctor who has her own career and who has made news with her frank television discussions on euthanasia. The second Mrs. Pinter, Lady Antonia Fraser, a well-known historical biographer, created a sensation with the divorce from her MP husband, a sensation compounded by the highly publicized indignant reaction of Pinter's first wife, Vivien Merchant, a talented actress who had appeared in many of Pinter's plays.

Both dramatists insist on the personal and professional necessity of disclaiming literary analyses that would classify and label their work. Yet recurrences of stylistic and thematic patterns in Pinter's dramas are obvious. There is general critical acceptance of the classification of his work as comedies of menace, comedies of intrigue, and poetic dramas. Even when interpretations have been, at best, conflicting and, at worst, strained to incredulity, the presence of rooms, intruders or menaces, cryptic language, pauses and silences pervades his dramatic situations and provides a consistency of style and structure.

Although not as reluctant as Pinter to talk about his work, Stoppard, too, has expressed disclaimers of meanings and ideas. Insisting on the difficulty of endorsing or discouraging particular theories, he has rejected those questions that demand "yes" and "no" answers. What is very important to him even when it puts off most people is "that there is very often *no* single, clear statement in my plays. What there is, is a series of conflicting statements made by conflicting characters, and they tend to play a sort of infinite leap-frog. You know, an argument, a refutation, then a rebuttal of the refutation, then a counter-rebuttal, so that there is never any point in this intellectual leap-frog at which I feel *that* is the speech to stop it on, *that* is the last word."[4]

Stoppard, however, provided some basis for classification of his plays. There are the "nuts and bolts" comedies, such as *After Magritte,* which are contentless as far as ideas are concerned. Then there are those plays in which ideas are debated—ideas about identity and existence in *Rosencrantz and Guildenstern Are Dead,* moral philosophy in *Jumpers,* art in *Travesties,* unionism in *Night and Day,* and love in *The Real Thing.* The wedding of ideas and high comedy in these dramas results in what Stoppard has identified as high comedies of ideas.

Most of his shorter pieces for radio, television, and stage fall into the former grouping and his long stage plays into the latter.

In still another interview, Stoppard stated: "I tend to write plays which consist of two voices disputing something, though naturally and obviously each voice is a separate aspect of myself. And it's an endless debate. I don't expect one voice suddenly to produce a final statement. It's a continuing process which results in plays as far as I'm concerned."[5]

The contradicting process, basic to both Pinter and Stoppard, happens in Pinter's plays as a psychological conflict in each character, a conflict between an inner reality struggling to remain private and those situations compelling its verbal expression. Stoppard's contradictions, however, are dramatized through brilliant debates between characters in which language juggling has been perfected into an art. Metaphors for this juggling are obvious in the coin tossing in *Rosencrantz and Guildenstern Are Dead* and in the acrobatics of *Jumpers*.

In an article, "Something to Declare," Stoppard has explained his style of contradictions further, taking it to its ultimate Beckettian end. "Beckett qualifies as he goes along. He picks up a proposition and then dismantles and qualifies each part of its structure as he goes along, until he nullifies what he started out with. Beckett gives me more pleasure than I can express because he always ends up with a man surrounded by the wreckage of a proposition he had made in confidence only two minutes before."[6]

Although critically acclaimed for their revolutionary stage language and Beckettian styles, Pinter and Stoppard exhibit sharp differences in their stage language, for Pinter is the master of the unspoken and Stoppard of the spoken word. The famous Pinter pauses, silences, and taut minimalist language that express the psychological fragmentation of character contrast sharply with the rich torrents of verbal play the Stoppardian character creates from the chaos and sterility of the world around him. Furthermore, Beckettian situations in both writers are handled with vast differences. The "no-man's land" of Pinter's carefully guarded character interiors contrasts with the accessibility of Stoppard's characters. Pinter's people fight desperately against threats to and intrusions on their privacy, whereas Stoppard's talk freely and, indeed, act out their fantasies.

In his narrative style, Pinter achieves suspense by withholding explanatory detail and action, whereas Stoppard crowds his plots with vividly detailed images and fast-paced action sequences. The static nature of Pinter's plots and the somewhat frenetic activity of Stoppard's present sharp contrasts. Structurally Pinter works with a conventionally clear-cut beginning, middle, and end, even when his character enigmas remain unresolved. Stoppard begins with divergent possibilities for a plot, one of which emerges as important and usually contains the resolution of the enigma or problem of the play. This plot pattern is particularly evident in the short comedies such as *After Magritte, The Real Inspector Hound,* and *Artist Descending the Staircase.*

Both dramatists have for their hallmarks easily identifiable beginnings, Pinter's perhaps more so than Stoppard's. Two or more people, standing or sitting in a room and being intruded on by strangers or threatened by some menace, characterize a Pinteresque plot from his very first play, *The Room.* A typical opening scene in a Stoppard play is an exotic, Magritte-like scene in which characters and their context are disjoined, hostile, or out of harmony with each other, in the manner of a dadaist painting.

Most pronounced among their differences, however, is the subject matter. Pinter's is drawn from his close observations of unspectacular people around him, to whom he gives a psychological mythology. They consist of slum landlords and tenants, hired killers, members of the fashion industry, models, philosophy professors, and middle-aged couples whose marriages have gone stale. Stoppard's subject matter derives from other writers and from personalities of history. Sophocles' *Philoctetes,* Arthur Miller's *Death of a Salesman,* Robert Bolt's *Flowering Cherry,* Shakespeare's *Hamlet* and *Macbeth,* Wilde's *The Importance of Being Earnest,* Beckett's *Waiting for Godot,* T. S. Eliot's "The Love Song of J. Alfred Prufrock," Joyce's *Ulysses,* Duchamp's *Nude Descending a Staircase,* Jasper Johns, Magritte, Tristan Tzara, Henry Carr, George Moore, and Lenin are but some of the sources and subjects of his plays.

Finally, a comparison of the two writers should note an ironic coincidence in their professional careers. Having written an impressive number of plays that could loosely be described as absurdist, both have written their latest plays in more conventional terms. The pause-ridden enigmas of Pinter and the Magritte-like situations of Stoppard have, in *Betrayal* and *Night and Day* respectively, given way to a realism/naturalism of content, language, and general style. In their assessments of these two plays, critics have called attention to what seems to them artistic self-betrayal. Indeed, both plays, ironically, are about betrayals of various sorts: marital, political, and professional.

In yet another coincidence, Stoppard's *The Real Thing* and Pinter's *Old Times* opened in New York in January 1984 with both dramatists in the United States for the occasion. With Jeremy Irons and Glenn Close in the former and Anthony Hopkins, Marsha Mason, and Jane Alexander in the latter, the fine productions, directed by Mike Nichols and Kenneth Frankel respectively, provided a much-needed brightening of a jaded New York theater season.

In acknowledging the differences between Stoppard and Pinter, Mel Gussow of the *New York Times* contends that "one must also affirm that they stand apart from many of their peers in their achievement of a universality." Comparing them with John Osborne and Arnold Wesker, socially relevant English playwrights whose subject matter dates them, Gussow refers to the fact that "early plays by Stoppard and Pinter are as fresh today as when they were written."[7]

Chapter Three

Enter a Free Man:
Man in Chains

Written in about three months in 1960 when Stoppard was twenty-three and still writing theater reviews, *Enter a Free Man,* his first play, was not produced on stage in London until 1968, a year after *Rosencrantz and Guildenstern Are Dead* had brought him instant fame. The play has a history of changes preceding its appearance on the London stage, including those of its title. Shown on ITV in 1963, it "appeared in Hamburg in 1964 under a title which translated as *The Spleen of Riley. . . .*" The reception in Hamburg, according to the author, "was applauded downstairs and booed upstairs."[1] Attributing the booing to the audience's expectation of either an angry or an absurd drama, Stoppard remarked that "when confronted with this splendid piece of boulevard kitchen sink," they "quite understandably booed."[2]

An announcement of the Oxford pre-London production of the play referred to this "new modern comedy" with still another title, *Home and Dry.* Commenting on the play as "The Flowering Death of a Salesman," and calling the work "phoney because it's a play written about other people's characters," the author admitted also to "a great deal of gratitude and affection, and a certain amount of embarrassment" in his feelings about it. "I don't think it's a very true play, in the sense that I feel no intimacy with the people I was writing about. It works pretty well as a play, but it's actually phoney. . . ."[4] Stoppard's reference to both Robert Bolt's *The Flowering Cherry* and Arthur Miller's *Death of a Salesman* has invited the inevitable comparisons, even to the similarity of names between Linda Riley (the daughter in Stoppard's play) and Linda Loman (the wife in Miller's).

In the realistic tradition of the conventional family problem play, *Enter a Free Man* joins a long line of domestic comedies that date back to Ibsen, whose likable but ne'er-do-well Hjalmer Ekdahl in *The Wild Duck* escapes from his own limitations into his illusions. Variations of this character are central to many major American dramas such as *The Glass Menagerie* by Williams, *Death of a Salesman* by Miller, *The Iceman Cometh* by O'Neill, and *Who's Afraid of Virginia Woolf?* by Albee.

In Stoppard's play the American dream—the persistent theme of so much American literature—is transmuted into the English dream. One is constantly reminded of this by the Rule Britannia chime clock in the Riley home that rings out at monotonous intervals in the domestic routines of the family. An antihero by default—in the long-standing tradition of the *miles gloriosus* comic figure—George Riley, Stoppard's Willy Loman, finds his release from the monotony of domestic life in his quixotic inventions of chime clocks, bottle openers, indoor plumbing for plants, and—the latest—a reusable envelope gummed on both sides of the flap. Like the illusions of the Ekdahls, the Wingfields, and the Lomans, his dreams of becoming rich and thereby acquiring some dignity are never realized.

The events of the play are simple. George Riley, as many times in the past, is leaving home, this time for good he says, to develop his latest invention into a financial success. Arriving at the local pub, he announces his intention to assorted companions, one of whom humors him in his illusion by offering to help with the financing. Using a double set, Stoppard alternates the action of the play conventionally between scenes in the pub and those at the Riley home, much as Arthur Miller did in his play. At the Riley home, Constance (Riley calls her Persephone, Percy for short) and daughter Linda engage in dialogue about the failures of both father and daughter. Linda's failures involve liaisons with men who eventually marry someone else or are already married. Both women work, the daughter keeping Riley supplied with spending money, since he is too lazy even to register for government assistance. All three family members feel imprisoned in a domestic situation that holds little promise for change. When Riley's scheme fails and he returns home to resume his routine existence, he acquiesces silently to Linda's plea that he at least register for the dole. The play ends on this note.

"A man is born free and everywhere he is in chains." Quoting from Rousseau's *Social Contract* as he enters the pub, Riley isn't sure of the author of his pronouncement, but he is sure of himself as its living embodiment. On the most obvious level, his chains are domestic, but in a deeper sense they are his own personal limitations, which no one recognizes more than does his wife. At one point she admits to Linda a partial responsibility for George's present financial state. Many years earlier in his aversion to remaining in a family business that may have provided them with some measure of financial security, she had encouraged him in his desire to leave that business: "The business was temporary for ten, eleven years. It would have been temporary all his life. If he was going to be a failure anyway, he was better off failing at something he wanted to succeed at. So he would be an inventor. It appealed to him. He liked to break . . . bounds. He got hold of a bit of enthusiasm. That was worth a lot."[5] Riley's situation is central to most of the plays of Stoppard, as characters break, or at least test, the bounds within which they find themselves held captive.

Like the wives and mothers of plays by O'Casey, Ibsen, and Arthur Miller, and like her mythological predecessor, Persephone is the life-sustaining force in the underworld that all inhabit. Providing necessary sympathy for the dilemma of her husband, she pleads with Linda to be charitable to Riley and reprimands her for not understanding Riley's laziness. Long-suffering, Persephone defends her husband:

You didn't mean anything because you don't know anything and you don't think. You don't ask yourself why—you don't ask yourself what it costs him to keep his belief in himself—to come back each time and start again—and it's worth keeping, it's the last thing he's got—but you don't know and you don't think and you don't ask. It costs him—everytime he comes back he loses a little face and he's lost a lot of face—to you he's lost all of it. You treat him like a crank lodger we've got living upstairs who reads fairy tales and probably wishes he lived in one, but he's ours and we're his, and don't you ever talk about him like that again. (*Spent*) You can call him the family joke, but it's our family. (*Pause.*) We're still a family. (67–68)

Persephone's anger resembles Linda Loman's anguish in Miller's play. "Is this his reward—to turn around at the age of sixty-three and find his sons, who he loved better than his life, one a philandering bum. . . ."[6]

Complementing the parallels between the dreams of success of Stoppard's Riley and Miller's Loman and between the wives in the two plays are the similarities between the daughter in one and the sons in the other. The once very close ties between father and child are recalled during a family row as Riley reminds Linda of the past when she went for walks with him and "had FAITH." She replies, "Noddy, Mickey Mouse, Fairy Annual—all my old books I had when I was a kid . . ." (62). When George is unmoved by her taunts, she turns a deaf ear to his childlike fantasy about coming back in a Rolls Royce so that "you'll believe me again and it'll be happy again" (63). In a similar father-son situation, Willy Loman needs the faith and love of Biff. Dreams of success by both fathers are the means to this end.

For both Riley and Loman, symbols of those dreams dominate the mood of the play. Willy's are the flute, the refrigerator, the automobile, the home, even the insurance money that he hopes will enable Biff to do something with himself; for Riley the symbols are his many inventions. Willy dies with his dream; George continues to live with his tattered dignity.

Its resemblances to Miller's play notwithstanding, Stoppard's is different in one major respect. The strong social criticism dominating *Death of a Salesman* is very weak in *Enter a Free Man.* Whenever social comment does occur, it takes the form of the absurdist dialogue of Beckett, Ionesco, and Pinter. It is conspicious by its resemblance to the stichomythic dialogue of early Pinter plays such as *The Birthday Party* and *The Dumbwaiter.* For example, complaining about the general state of things, Riley places the blame for moral deterioration on people wanting something for nothing. "No wonder the country is going to the dogs. Personal enterprise sacrificed to bureaucracy. No pride, no patriotism. The erosion of standards, the spread of mediocrity, the decline of craftsmanship and the betrayal of the small inventor" (15). Sterile platitudes abound as in most absurdist plays. Harry and Carmen, pub companions who humor George in his fantasies, respond in like manner:

HARRY: It's terrible, really. I blame youth.

CARMEN: Education.

HARRY: The Church is out of touch.

CARMEN: The family is not what it was.

HARRY: It's the power of the unions.

CARMEN: The betrayal of the navy.

HARRY: Ban the bomb.

CARMEN: Spare the rod.

HARRY: I'm all right, Jack.

CARMEN: The little man goes to the wall.

HARRY: Supermarkets.

CARMEN: Everything's plastic. (15)

Ben and Gus in Pinter's *The Dumbwaiter* go through similar absurdist-style dialogue as they wait for their victim to arrive. In Pinter's *The Birthday Party,* produced several years before *Enter a Free Man,* McCann and Goldberg reflect those societal forces that have forced Stanley into his present condition:

> MCCANN: You'll be rich.
>
> GOLDBERG: You'll be adjusted.
>
> MCCANN: You'll be our pride and joy.[7]

Pinter's stichomythic lines surrealistically create the sterility of the characters while expressing the prevailing societal platitudes. Stoppard's naturalistic language, on the other hand, creates a dominantly comic effect.

In addition to the dialogues, there are long monologues in this first play of Stoppard's that evoke passages from Pinter, more in substance than in style, however. For example, the cornflakes and fried bread conversations between Meg and Petey Boles and Stanley Webber in *The Birthday Party* are suggested in Riley's lengthy account of his domestic prison:

My wife and I and Linda, we get up in the morning and the water is cold . . . fried bread and sausage and tea . . . the steam in the kitchen and the smell of it all and the springs are broken in my chair. . . . Linda goes to sell things . . . in Woolworth's . . . cosmetics and toilet things, and we wash up when the kettle boils again . . . and I go to my room . . . and sit there . . . with my pencils and my workbench. . . . And when I came down this morning there she was, just watering the flowers, from a jug, as usual. (34–35)

But in spite of the Pinteresque touches in the monologues and dialogues, *Enter a Free Man,* as described by Stoppard, is kitchen-sink realism, a style Stoppard abandons until it reappears in *Night and Day* nearly twenty years later in much more sophisticated form.

This first play by Stoppard does, however, begin stylistic and thematic qualities that have become hallmarks of his other work. George Riley is a simplified antecedent of the complex Rosencrantz and Guildenstern, Moon, George Moore, Joyce, Lenin, and others in later works who insist on questioning things or escaping from the chains that bind.

Chapter Four
Scratching a Living: Short Stories

Having sold a year's option on *A Walk on the Water* for a hundred pounds at a time when he "had never had ten quid in a lump sum before,"[1] Stoppard told *Theatre Quarterly* interviewers that he continued writing theater reviews for *Scene* to be able to stay in London: "One room, scratching a living, not writing much apart from a few short stories—three of which Faber eventually published."[2]

The three stories are the only short fiction he has published. They stand apart from his other work in their strongly personal content and style. All three appeared in an anthology, *Stories by New Writers* (1964). A fourth story submitted with the other three was not accepted. This story, about Marilyn Monroe's death, was later written as a television play, *"M" Is for Moon Among Other Things,* produced by BBC in 1967.

"Reunion" tells the story of a man meeting a woman from his past. Although named "he" and "the woman," the two characters create a highly personalized, intimate mood in their responses to each other. "Life, Times: Fragments" and "The Story" are even more personalized as they are told by a first-person narrator. Both draw on Stoppard's experiences and observations as journalist and author.

"Reunion"

Suggesting the style of Pinter's "Silence" and "Landscape" (staged five years after the publication of Stoppard's story), a man and a woman attempt a conversation in which their small talk sporadically and dangerously skirts their separate truths. The conversation veers to the subject of language, which, when accurately timed "at the right pitch and in a silence worthy of it, would nudge the universe into gear."[3]

The man uses the example of a "public place dedicated to silence, like the reading room at the British Museum" (123), which must be violated by the sound of a certain word. Breaking the silence would be "a monstrous, unspeakable intrusion after which nothing can be the same for the man who does it" (123). Earlier he had thought that picking up a bottle and smashing it against the stone sink would relieve him sufficiently so that he "could last out the night or until his arm got tired. It was one of the things you knew without ever doing them, and he could stand up in a public library and scream, now, the word, and he would be all right" (122). In his childhood he nearly had had the experience when he knocked his prayer book off the ledge and it had gone off like a pistol shot. "I reckon for two seconds everything intrusive to myself flew out of me, and then back. It's something like that" (124). The dislocation is an experience that many of Stoppard's characters undergo.

Throughout the conversation there is reference to the woman's husband (or lover) who may come home any time and find the man there. The increasing urgency of the man is externalized in his comment that he misses her "approaching down busy streets, and eating together and saving things to tell you and having things saved for me . . ." (124). But these are memories he can easily dismiss. There is only one that persists, and that one is "always you in bed." He insists that "we could be very good. . . . We nearly were" and evokes from her the advice to find "a girl and have a marvellous affair and you'll be all right" (124,125). She finally accedes to his assertion that her lover/husband won't be coming back; whether she does so to silence him or whether it is the truth remains ambiguous. With her "Oh, shut up," his body disconnected, "and it took a long time, stairs and streets later, before he got a hold on it again, without, as always, having murdered anybody" (125). Stoppard's description of the sexual reunion is precise and minimal.

The story of the seduction by a former lover of a middle-aged woman who still "gave off summer colours all the year round" (121) is a finished piece of writing. Its detached, yet sensuous language, suggests the evocative, unspoken communication in the plays of Pinter. The middle-aged couple converse in banalities until out of the unspoken silence a disrupting word, in this case, "fire," emerges and catalyzes those banalities into action. Like Eliot's Prufrock, whose upper-class civility and middle-aged indecisiveness keep him from "squeezing the universe into a ball," the man here seems paralyzed until that word appears. Until the appearance of the word, the man and woman quibble about his promising not to come to visit her.

When he insists on knowing whether her life is better, she responds that it is different. And grasping for a sharper definition of *different,* he "felt it [the earth level, 'a word' that he held] slipping and he grabbed himself silent" (122). Language, like sex, becomes the very subject of the story. Their conversation then takes a religious turn. The right word shouted in silence jumps to the "Word of God," which, for the man, creates a new dimension, a religious faith. "One would have to avoid a billion permutations of phonetics and chance unawares on the one sound which is the Word" (123). When the woman suggests *fire,* the flow of language in the man is released:

"Pafflid," he said, as happy as he had ever been in his whole life, "brilge, culp, matrap, drinnop, quelp, trid, crik, christ," he said, "I do love you, please try, don't" and willed a whole embrace into the finger-touch on her bare arm which moved away unalarmed, and then completed the destruc-tion—"I can't stop, like that." (123–24)

The language released here suggests the nonsense schoolboy language (Dogg) of Stoppard's later plays, language that has meaning only for those few who know it. It is life-giving and communicative when conventional language fails.

In "Reunion" language is all, whether as a catalyst for the sexual reunion or as a metaphor for the urgency of meaningful communica-tion. The contrast between the early banalities and the later fantasy language supports the latter.

Stoppard's other stories, "Life, Times: Fragments" and "The Story" take on an intensely autobiographical cast, as "Reunion" does not. Both stories are about a journalist who finds himself in situations that have disillusioning consequences. Both stories, narrated in the first person, contain the most autobiographical subject matter of Stop-pard's work.

"Life, Times: Fragments"

Written in seven paragraphs, each a particular time segment in the life of a journalist turned writer, the story deals with that life from young adulthood to the writer's posthumous discovery by a critic who, although making his subject famous, makes himself even more so.

Stoppard's playing with language is immediate in the first frag-ment, in which the journalist erroneously reports that a body of a female crash victim had been identified. He felt sick until the woman whose death he reported actually died the next day. "In a funny way that made it all right,"[4] he reports.

In the last fragment another body, this time the body of the work of the writer, was "discovered by the most famous critic in the land. Picking up the suicide note, the critic found he could not put it down. 'Why,' he declared, unable to believe his luck, 'another one! It is my considered etcetera bitter humour Gogol agonized vision Kafkacetera etcetera. I have discovered the body,' he added, swiftly ransacking the furniture, 'of his work. That brings me up to five, with two possibles' " (130).

Between these first and last paragraphs of the story, the first-person narrator mentions being "slightly shameful about being twenty-five in the provinces" (126) and relates his rejection by the *Evening Standard* because he did not know the name of the foreign secretary. Both of these experiences are those Stoppard has talked about with interviewers. The autobiographical tone is obvious.

In the second time frame, he tells of an affair with a woman at Marbella, where at the age of twenty-seven he had given in to the lazy pleasures of sand, sea, and the favors of a wealthy woman.

In the next fragment he is thirty-four, and here the point of view shifts to third person. Stoppard begins the projection of the possible course of the journalist-cum-writer. Now he is a general who with cynical sophistication attempts to impress his lady by putting down major writers such as Stendhal, Balzac, Flaubert, Wilde, Henry James, and Thackeray. For the source of his cynicism, he quotes famous American critics: "Kafka is over-rated—read Edmund Wilson! Gatsby's a glorified and improbable anecdote—read Mencken! Hemingway's an adolescent philistine—read Dwight Macdonald!" (128). These references become significant at the end when a critic's discovery of the narrator-author's body of work brings him fame. Stoppard's irony undercuts the braggadocio of the general as he whispers hoarsely to his lady: "I will do it . . . and it will be for you. . . . *I am—I feel—seminal!*" (128). The double entendre, as in "Reunion," closes the general's pompous attempt to impress. Unlike her counterpart in "Reunion," however, the lady rejects his advances.

At fifty the narrator once more assumes the first person. Depressed by his lack of success, he considers picking up the threads again, but then recalls that "they get younger all the time. Perhaps I'm the oldest sub in London" (129). As in "Reunion," a religious note intrudes in a journalist's parody of the Lord's Prayer: "Give us this day our daily press, and forgive us our intrusions into private grief. . . . Lead us into sensation and deliver us from libel for thine. . . ." Finally, after his 127th consecutive rejection slip, the writer offers himself to the Lord, who heard him and sent an angel to add still another rejection to the long list: "The Lord thanks you for your contribution but regrets that it is not quite suitable for the kingdom of heaven" (129).

The posthumous discovery of the writer-suicide only adds to the depression caused by the rejection by the *Evening Standard,* by his lady friend, and then by God. The cynical seasoned critic was wont to quip, "Oh yes, it was I who discovered old So-and-so, you know. I just opened the door and there he was" (130).

The story is a review of the journalist's life up to the age of twenty-seven (an age close to Stoppard's when he wrote the piece) and a disheartening view of what the rest of it could be. Each of the time periods has its moods: the terrible sick feeling occasioned by erroneous reporting, the shame at being rejected by the *Evening Standard,* the somnolence of a life of pleasure on an Italian beach, the cynicism of the critic, the troubled thinking of the rejected writer, and, finally, the irony-fantasy of the posthumous discovery of his body of work.

Although told in fragments, the story's time progression is linear, as with age the journalist-writer disintegrates psychologically and artistically. References to death and to the body at the beginning and end form a fitting framework for the progressive moods.

In a more sophisticated manner, this deceptively fragmented structure occurs in the first chapter of Stoppard's novel and in many of his dramas.

"The Story"

A straightforward narrative, without the evocative language of "Reunion" or the intriguing structure and voice-shifts of "Life, Times: Fragments," "The Story" concerns a journalist dispatched to cover a story in a seaside town. While waiting to get a line on a scrap-metal theft and some other stories, he chances on still another news item involving a master in a public school, who, in teaching a little girl to swim, fondled her and was arrested. Since it was his first offense, he was fined twenty-five pounds and released.

In selling the insignificant item to the press services, however, the journalist, thinking it not worth a man's reputation, discovers that as services picked the story up, details were added that enlarged it way beyond its importance. One day when he and his colleagues are having a drink, they discuss the master's suicide in London. In a detached yet ironically emotional way, Stoppard's story ends with the journalist counting a total of three pounds, two shillings, and sixpence he had received for the news item. The absence of journalistic regard for the human element could hardly have been more condemnatory than the narrator's final comment: "I don't know what I spent it on. It got mixed up with my other money and at the end of the month I was broke as usual" (136). Stoppard's concern with ethical problems of journalists is dramatized with intellectual complexity in *Night and Day* (1978), but it is a concern that was with him as early as 1964.

Chapter Five
Lord Malquist and Mr. Moon: A Novel

If *Enter a Free Man* indicates the broad directions Stoppard's writing takes, his only novel, *Lord Malquist and Mr. Moon,* published in 1966, serves as an explicit guide to his dramas. Indeed, Kenneth Tynan sees the novel as a work in which Stoppard can be read at his philosophically purest.[1] And Stoppard himself must have had a similar attitude at the time of the novel's publication. He spoke of "scanning the papers for his dream book reviews," finding, instead, the *Observer*'s rave review of *Rosencrantz and Guildenstern Are Dead.* "So I was slightly taken aback. . . . *Lord Malquist and Mr. Moon,* which went down particularly well in Venezuela," sold nearly as many copies there as in England. "Only since Faber have said they'll bring it out again have I begun to suspect that it wasn't all that good."[2]

In a variation of the picaresque tradition, *Lord Malquist and Mr. Moon* is the story of the title characters, the former an eighteenth-century gentleman who finds the chaos of modern life unbearable and, consequently, withdraws from it with style. With meticulous attention to his dress and behavior, Malquist rides about the automobile-ridden streets of modern central London in a malquist, the last horse-drawn carriage, as he himself is the ninth and last earl. In addition to his wife, Laura, who is habitually escorted from the Ritz Hotel in an inebriated state and who eventually frees Moon from his sexual impotence, Malquist's household boasts a butler named Birdboot (a recurring name in later plays), a lionlike dog named Rollo, and a falcon.

To record for posterity his pronouncements on life, Malquist employs Mr. Moon, and the two go "Boswelling it" in London on the day of the funeral of the last national hero (Churchill, presumably). This contemporary Samuel Johnson and James Boswell ride in style through London, occasionally running over a person in their way.

At the time he is hired by Malquist, Moon is involved in writing a history of the world, his efforts meeting with little success. Like

Riley of *Enter a Free Man,* he is a failure, and his taking on the additional task of Boswelling for Malquist only creates enormous difficulties for him. To complicate matters, his wife Jane (named Fertility
Jane by one of her two cowboy admirers) is sexually incompatible
with Moon but nymphomaniacal with others. She enjoys the atten-
tions of two cowboys, Jasper Jones and Long John Slaughter, and,
later, Malquist himself. In addition to this improbable Moon
ménage, there is Marie, the maid, accidentally shot dead by one of
the cowboys attempting to eliminate his rival.

The loose plot involves Malquist and Moon in the carriage driving
madly through the labyrinthine streets of London near St. James'
Park, as the former dictates his philosophy of life to Moon. His statements comprise a substantial number of attitudes, wittily shaped,
that will reappear in Stoppard's plays.

Moon, meantime, seems to be losing his grasp on himself and his
own ambitious historical project. Indeed, he carries a bomb with him
that ticks its way through the novel, reminding him of the means by
which he will free the world from its chaos when the time comes.
One is reminded of Bely's novel *St. Petersburg,* a similarly expression-
istic, episodic novel, in which a revolutionist is involved with a ticking bomb that explodes at the end. Moon's bomb, however, is
accidentally touched off at the conclusion, and Moon is killed. The
novel ends with neither Malquist's life nor Moon's history having
been recorded.

Helping to define the traditional Christian context and the contemporary social context are two of the novel's most bizarre characters. The Risen Christ rides into town on his donkey, and O'Hara,
the black Jewish-Irish-Catholic coachman, drives the Malquists' carriage. Along with the cowboys on their horses (or mares) and the carriage rides of Malquist and Moon, these two characters create bizarre
spectacles on the landscape of modern London. Most farcical of all the
street scenes, perhaps, is that in which the dead body of Marie, the
maid, wrapped in a blanket on the back of the Risen Christ's donkey,
becomes a part of the funeral procession of the national hero. The
novel abounds in similarly absurd scenes of characters dadaistically
wrenched from their customary contexts. (The dadaist influence is
suggested, in fact, in the name of the cowboy Jasper Jones, a parodic
use of the name of the artist Jasper Johns.)

If Malquist has chosen to withdraw from the chaos of modern life,
he does remain in it as a detached spectator and, also, as a spectacle

for the crowds he is contemptuous of. As such, he illustrates Stoppard's definition of the new hero. His anachronistic eccentricities of dress and behavior and his rejection of modern London enable him to withstand the vulgarities of the age, such as the phoney urban cowboys and the twentieth-century ethnic-religious stereotypes of O'Hara and the Risen Christ. In turn, he provides farcical spectacles for Londoners when his falcon and his lionlike dog (Rollo) attract notice as one dashes after the other.

The spectacles involve others of the Moon and Malquist households in a succession of scenes in which anachronisms converge, such as the scene involving the cowboys, the falcon, and Rollo:

With a sob Slaughter went for his gun. It fell on the ground and bounced and there was a roar from a .45 as Jasper outdrew him and shot himself in the leg. Jasper cursed and sat down. Fast as a rattlesnake Long John scooped up his gun and shot Jasper in the stomach and started to run across the Square past Jasper who was dying on his knees. A mountain lion with a flamingo in its mouth streaked across in front of him and seemed to leap over the backs of the crowd; and beyond, a pink coach was rattling down the Mall towards him.[3]

Even sexual activity becomes a spectacle as Malquist, Moon, and the Risen Christ watch Fertility Jane's self-induced orgasm, the result of a question she puts to Malquist about what Scotsmen wear under their kilts:

"I *know* Scotsmen, they don't let themselves be coddled up. They're *big*. They're big brawny giants with powerful muscles straining taut, striding about in their kilts"—she had her thighs squeezed together, her eyes closed now, head lolling back, a priestess incantating through the fumes of sacrifice—"in their *kilts,* with their great strong legs rippling hard as knotted cord. . . ."
                                                              . . .
The ninth earl caught her as she fell.
"Jane, are you all right?"
"Lovely, darling, just lovely. Can I have a cigarette?" (61–62)

Malquist provides the postsexual cigarette, Moon draws her bath at her request, and Jane engages the Risen Christ in some conversation. With her nymphomania and her husband's impotence—indeed, male impotence in general—Jane anticipates the wife of the philosopher George Moore in *Jumpers*. She, like the other bizarre characters, must create her own context and her own style. Style provides meaning in an otherwise meaningless world. Malquist's oft-repeated dictum that nothing—"rien"—is the history of the world is illustrated in the divergent style of each character. His definition is precise: " 'Such utter disregard for the common harmonies of life,' complained the ninth earl. 'I look around me and I recoil from such disorder. . . . Since we cannot hope for order let us withdraw with style from the chaos' " (21).

If each character and his/her actions are defined by a disjointedness with contemporary context, so is the very structure of the novel a deliberately disjointed one. A series of six unrelated episodes, each a dadaist-like painting, constitute the first chapter, titled "Dramatis Personae and Other Coincidences." The remaining five chapters gradually fill in the gaps among these scenes until they converge in the accidental bombing death of Moon at the end.

Listening to Malquist, Moon, too, is educated into the absurdity of things, particularly regarding Malquist's pronouncement that style is all. "There is nothing else" (63). Reminiscent of Oscar Wilde, Malquist writes to Moon: "I would rather my book were unread than ungraceful . . ." (68). Indeed, the contemporary hero is defined by his style, rather than by his action, as in the past:

As you will have realized when your receive this, I write to you on the day of the death of a national hero. I mention this because I think it makes an appropriate moment for the commencement of our venture. I sense that the extravagant mourning exacted from and imposed upon a sentimental people is the last flourish of an age whose criteria of greatness are no longer applicable. . . . For this reason, his death might well mark a change in the heroic posture—to that of the Stylist, the spectator as hero, the man of inaction who would not dare roll up his sleeves [Prufrock] for fear of creasing the cuffs. (79)

Halfway between the old hero and the new, Moon, like T. S. Eliot's J. Alfred Prufrock, is as indecisive as Malquist is decisive. Allusions to Eliot's hero abound in the novel. Like him, Moon must prepare the face to meet the faces. He had to "abandon his interview to prepare a face to acknowledge the loyalty of a populace who had turned out to line the streets for him . . . (11). His self-consciousness is most acute. Like Prufrock, he "had tried to pin the image of an emotion against the wall but he did not have the words to transfix it" (23). Eliot in his poem talks about people measuring out their lives with coffee spoons, and Stoppard's Moon "did not have the words to translate a certain fear about something as real as a coffee-pot, only not a coffee-pot and he did not even have the words to formulate that" (23).

Then there is the variation on familiar lines from "The Love Song of J. Alfred Prufrock":

> (That is not it at all,
> that is not what I meant at all.
> But when I've got it in a formulated phrase, when I've
> got it formulated, sprawling on a pin, when it is pinned
> and wriggling on the wall, then how should I begin. . . .?)
> *And how should you presume?*
>
> (23–24)

Words, like sex, fail Moon. To his maid, Marie, Moon says: "I mean, your breasts are so *little* and—*That is not what I meant at all*. You're so young, so quiet, and calm and sweet and quiet and young . . ." (27). In a paraphrase of Prufrock's subconscious ruminations, Moon "was trying to frame a question that would take in all the questions, and elicit an answer that would be all the answers, but it kept coming out so simple that he distrusted it" (30). There is even a reference to the close of Eliot's poem as Moon thinks about clutching "at straws but what good's a brick to a drowning man?" (52). At one point, he quotes almost verbatim from Eliot as he tells the Risen Christ that his "whole life is waiting for the questions to which I have prepared answers, and looking for the answer to the overwhelming question. . . . Oh do not ask what is it, let us go and make our visit" (46–47). Moon's Prufrockian indecisiveness is summed up in a conversation with O'Hara: "I cannot commit myself to either side of a question. . . . Because if you attach yourself to one or the other you disappear into it" (54).

Moon's verbal, logical, and sexual impotences converge in a scene in which he claims his marital rights from Jane. In response she throws perfume bottles and other cosmetic objects at him, and his body feels like "one big lung. The spring unwound itself, proportion was re-established. He rocked blind in the great calm, his mouth loose, his legs gone. He knew what it was to solve the world" (64). Shortly afterward he abandons his abortive beginning of the history of the world. The disparity between the romantic world about which Eliot's Prufrock fantasizes and the monotony of the real world in

which people measure out their lives in coffee spoons cripples Prufrock for any kind of decisive action, and he drowns in his retreat from
life. Similarly, Moon says that his "emotional bias towards the reac-
tionary and my intellectual bias towards the radical do not survive
each other and are each interred by my aesthetic revulsion of their
respective adherents . . ." (79). Like Prufrock and like the debating
characters to appear in Stoppard's plays, Moon engages in self-argu-
ments that cancel each other. Like George Riley with his inventions,
Moon could not actively pursue his goal, either his history of the
world or his Boswelling of Malquist. He dies a failure. He has even
lost control of the bomb, and it accidentally explodes. Unlike Malquist, Moon is tortured by his quest for meanings and has no detachment or style to sustain him when meanings fail.

Malquist and Moon can be seen as a doppelgänger character, a double torn equally between certainty and doubt. The Churchillian man
of action becomes extinct on this day of the burial of the last hero.
He ceases to exist but the spectator-stylist not only survives but survives with an elegance because he has defined his context and,
thereby, his style and meaning. He has triumphed in his withdrawal
from the chaos of the times. The heroes of Stoppard's dramas are successful failures who appear in his works as early as George Riley in
Enter a Free Man and Lord Malquist in the novel.

When asked by Ronald Hayman about T. S. Eliot and J. Alfred
Prufrock, Stoppard replied: "There are cetain things written in English which make me feel as a diabetic must feel when the insulin
goes in. Prufrock and Beckett are the twin syringes of my diet, my
arterial system."[4]

If the injection from Eliot is strong in his novel, that from Beckett
in his next play, *Rosencrantz and Guildenstern Are Dead,* is even
stronger.

Chapter Six

Rosencrantz and Guildenstern Are Dead: Entitled to Some Direction

As with *Enter a Free Man, Rosencrantz and Guildenstern Are Dead* underwent a series of mutations to its present form. It was begun during a Ford Foundation cultural picnic for promising young playwrights held in Berlin, Germany, from May to October 1964. Similar to the Eugene O'Neill annual summer workshops in Connecticut, the event provided writers, among whom was Tom Stoppard, opportunity to write and to have their work performed. Originally a one-act comedy in verse, the play bore the title *Rosencrantz and Guildenstern Meet King Lear* and was performed by young English amateur actors.

Upon his return to London, Stoppard rewrote the play in prose and changed the title. When the Royal Shakespeare Company's twelve-month option on the play expired, the Oxford Theatre Group received permission to perform it as a fringe theater production at the Edinburgh Festival in 1966. Stoppard himself arrived in Edinburgh, when the production was undergoing difficulties, to revise repetitious portions. The rest is history, as Ronald Bryden's enthusiastic review of the play catapulted it and its author to the attention of the National Theatre at the Old Vic, which bought the script and produced it in April 1967. "The *Sunday Times* called it 'the most important event in the British professional theatre of the last nine years'; that is, since Harold Pinter's *The Birthday Party.*"[1]

In a *Theatre Quarterly* interview, Stoppard talked about his two leading characters as "these two guys who in Shakespeare's context don't really know what they're doing. The little they are told is mainly lies, and there's no reason to suppose that they ever find out why they are killed."[2] He added that the exploration of their situation in the early 1960s with the "right combination of specificity and vague generality"[3] was both interesting to him as playwright and

29

conducive to the "many kinds of interpretation, all of them plausible, but none of them calculated."[4] Reviewers and critics were quick to mention the specific resemblances to Beckett's *Waiting for Godot* and to the plays of Pirandello.

But unlike Stoppard's first play, *Rosencrantz and Guildenstern Are Dead* is anything but imitative, for the two notoriously insignificant characters in the Shakespeare drama take on equally notorious significance in the games of language, ideas, and actions that they play wittily and brilliantly. In Stoppard's play, as central rather than peripheral characters, they explore matters of identity, role playing, meaning, fate, probability, and general problems of knowledge. Indeed, the fusion of the source and influences results in a wholly fresh play, which *Enter a Free Man* is not. In *Rosencrantz and Guildenstern Are Dead* Stoppard has successfully realized the combination of farce and ideas, resulting in what he has called a high comedy of ideas.

The first of the play's three acts opens with what seems an interminable scene of coin spinning by Rosencrantz and Guildenstern. They have spun ninety-two times, and each time the coins have come down heads. Guil's bag is nearly empty and Ros's bag is nearly full, reminiscent of the Beckettian character who transfers pebbles from one to the next of his four pockets after he tastes each, eventually finding one pretty much the same as the other. In the course of the spinning, Ros and Guil argue theories of probability by means of syllogistic thinking. Their conversation, occurring in a "place without any visible character," evokes the arid expanses of a Beckettian landscape, so that even when Claudius and Gertrude and their entourage appear, the sense of contextlessness permeates the play.

In his first monologue of any length, Guil recounts the tale of their having been summoned from Wittenburg to Elsinore by a messenger and having heard "for the last three minutes on the wind of a windless day . . . the sound of drums and flute. . . ."[5] Shortly thereafter, a Player and his tragedians appear in a ménage that includes a small boy, Alfred, along with a drummer, a horn-player, and a flutist. Two are pulling and pushing a cart with props and belongings. The action of the play is underway as Ros and the Player debate the cost of being spectators as opposed to the cost of participating in the action. Finally as the tragedians pick up their belongings as though to move on—again reminiscent of the Lucky-Pozzo duo in Beckett's *Waiting for Godot*—Guil, the intellectual of the pair, questions the Player regarding his destination, and they discover that all are headed for the court. Guil then, involving the Player in a game of coin spinning, wins by deception and is offered Alfred, the young boy, as payment. Stoppard's love of joking is illustrated as they discuss this possibility of a dramatic precedent as "no way to fill the theatres of Europe" (32). As the talk turns to plays in demand at the time, the Player insists on plays with blood, love, and rhetoric, with blood being the compulsory ingredient. The Player also mentions that he never takes off his costume, introducing the Pirandellian concept of role playing as reality.

Toward the end of the act Ophelia, Claudius, Gertrude, and Polonius appear briefly to greet the two friends of Hamlet and to inform them of the reason for their visit. When Ros and Guil are alone again, the former expresses his fear and confusion and wants to go home. After he has calmed Ros, Guil declares that, although they have no choice, they are at least presented with alternatives. In a world of uncertainties that cause Ros to lose his direction, there are only two certainties, that the only beginning is birth and the only ending is death. Accepting events as a determinant, Guil assures Ros that everything will come out all right. In response to Ros's question, "How long?" Guil replies: "Till events have played themselves out. There's a logic at work—it's all done for you, don't worry" (40). Guil's consolation of Ros concludes with a response to the latter's comment that spectatorship is bearable because of the "irrational belief that somebody interesting will come on in a minute" (41). Guil is aware of the "fine persecution—to be kept intrigued without ever being enlightened . . ." (41).

To acquire some practice in this new knowledge of themselves, Guil suggests that they play a game of questions, again evocative of the games Didi and Gogo play in Beckett's *Waiting for Godot*. The questions involve their identities, God, Hamlet, Gertrude, and Claudius. Ros thinks he hears music, and soon the pair of characters is interrupted by the Hamlet-Polonius scenes from Shakespeare in which Polonius comments about Hamlet's madness and Hamlet greets Rosencrantz and Guildenstern. The first act is the longest of the three, and the troubled questioning of the two men remains to be played out in full in the remaining acts.

The second act focuses on the Player and his tragedians as they interact with Ros and Guil and as they act out their traditional roles from Shakespeare's play. But it is only as Guil and Ros act out the knowledge of their roles that their roles take on the significance of their insignificance. Ros, however, rebels and insists that notice be taken of him. He is, like Gogo in Beckett's play, a person who feels the pain of things. Counteracting Ros's rebellion and Guil's questioning is the Player who never has to change into costume because he never changes out of it and who extracts significance from melodrama, a significance that it does not, in fact, contain. The Player's comments throughout the second act echo Pirandellian attitudes regarding art as a means of giving order and, therefore, meaning to life. "For all anyone knows, nothing is" (67). "One acts on assumptions" (67). By the end of the act Ros is convinced that they should go with Hamlet to England on the assumption that they'll be free. It is Guil who now questions, not that they should not come back, but that they should go. He is under the illusion that he has a choice in the events.

Act 3 is the shortest and the most action-packed. The debates and questions about identity, memory, meaning, and purpose have been more or less completed in the first two acts. It remains for them to be played out in the plot action. On board the ship on their way to England, Ros and Guil hear music and are surprised when the lids pop off the barrels on the ship and the Player with his tragedians emerges. Stoppard cleverly changes Shakespeare into Beckett here. (Beckett employs wastebins and urns in *Endgame* and *Play*).

When the pirates attack, Hamlet jumps into the left barrel, the players into the right one. Stoppard's placing of Ros and Guil in the middle barrel is a visual metaphor for their entrapment in the vise of events and for their occupation of center stage in the play.

The fast physical action is followed by the discovery of the letter that Hamlet has changed. Forming a menacing circle around Ros and Guil, the players symbolize the events that have trapped this most insignificant duo of Shakespearean characters. Guil quietly acknowledges the inexorability of events, while Ros expresses wonder at being important enough to have been part of a grand scheme right from the start.

After the noise and action subside, Hamlet has disappeared, and a ritual scene is enacted, Guil's attempted killing of the Player. Even this act is meaningless, as Guil discovers that the knife-blade is retractable. But the incident proves the Player's earlier argument that even death is a game that can be convincingly acted. The Player then in turn stabs the tragedians and disappears, as the stage lights come on, transforming the tragedians' bodies into the heap of corpses at the end of Shakespeare's tragedy. Playacting and real life events fuse. Their last words in the play—to each other—are "Rosen—? Guil—?" (125) and "Well, we'll know better next time. Now you see me, now you—" (126). The curtain falls on a tableau of court and corpses as in Shakespeare's play as the Norwegian ambassador and Horatio provide the concluding comments.

The two main characters, nicknamed Ros and Guil in the manner of Beckett's Gogo and Didi, can be seen either as separate characters or as a composite. The Player and his tragedians clearly suggest the Lucky-Pozzo duo of Beckett's play. A third composite, consisting of Hamlet, Polonius, Gertrude, Claudius, Horatio, and Fortinbras, can be seen as the Beckettian Godot for whom Gogo and Didi wait, to be satisfied only by the appearance of Godot's messenger, a small boy.

What is unknown, although anticipated by Beckett's two protagonists, is the known, but unanticipated, fact of "having come" in the lives of Ros and Guil. At various points throughout the play, Guil comforts himself and Ros with this sure fact of their existence: "A man standing in his saddle in the half-lit half-alive dawn banged on the shutters and called two names. He was just a hat and a cloak levitating in the grey plume of his own breath, but when he called we came. That much is certain—we came" (39).

Like the word games played by Didi and Gogo, question-and-answer games by Ros and Guil follow the coin spinning with which the play begins and which recurs at intervals throughout the play. They discuss the probabilities of the outcome of each spin, the uncertainties of their names and identities, and their reason for coming. All of the games—including the biggest of all, the game of life itself—are those in which man is confronted by his fate as was Oedipus. If, as Jan Kott contends, in modern tragedy fate has been replaced by history, Stoppard seems to assert that history has been replaced by an event, an insignificant event such as Ros and Guil's coming when their shutters had been rudely banged on in the half-lit and half-alive dawn by the messengers of the court.

Indeed, there is an interesting treatment in Kott's work *Shakespeare Our Contemporary* of the very matter of coin tossing and probability, which bears close resemblance to the game dramatized by Stoppard in act 1.

There is a machine for a game similar to tossing coins for "heads or tails." I put a coin on the table the way I like, with "heads" or "tails" on top. The machine does not see the coin, but it has to predict how I have put it. If it gives the right answer it wins. I inform the machine whether it has given the right answer. I put down the coin again, and so on. After a time the machine begins to win by giving the right answers more and more often. It has memorized and learned my system; it has deciphered me, as it were. . . .

There is a move by which I do not lose. I do not put the coin on the table, I do not choose, I simply toss it. I have given up the system, and left matters to chance. Now the machine and I have even chances. The possibility of win and lose, of "heads" or "tails" is the same. It amounts to fifty-fifty. The machine wanted me to treat it seriously, to play rationally with it, using a system, a method. But I do not want to. It is I who have now seen through the machine's method.[6]

Guil, the reasoning member of the duo, has been educated into the machine's methods and, consequently, has seen through them. He finally realizes that the only certainty he can have is that he is denied the explanation of who he is, why he is here, what significance he may have. The certainty of not knowing is at least the certainty gained since he and Ros were summoned to Elsinore. Throughout the play the return of the nagging questions are like the return of the small boy in *Waiting for Godot:* both are illusions that are swept away only by death. Beckettian phrases such as "not-knowing" and "not-being" recur in the last act of Stoppard's play in illustration of the certainty of this knowledge on the part of Guil. The small certainty of their deaths within the larger certainty of the inevitability of events is Guil's ultimate method of dealing with the machine of fate. As such, this knowledge is his way of choosing not to play with the machine on its own terms and, thus, provides him with some identity, significance, and dignity for which he and Ros anguish throughout the play. The melodramatic mime scene on board the ship in which Guil in earnest stabs the Player with a retractable knife conclusively illustrates the Player's contention that the melodrama of life contains only the significance that man, as Pirandellian and Beckettian role player, assigns to it. Reality has rent the veil of illusion, and Guil's education is complete.

Although Beckett's influence is dominant in Stoppard's reworking of *Hamlet,* Eliot remains an influence, but in a much more subdued form than in *Lord Malquist and Mr. Moon.* In moving Shakespeare's peripheral characters to the center of his own play, Stoppard deploys them as his still point, a recurring idea in Eliot's poetry. That still point involves the only certainty of the existence of Ros and Guil: that they were called and that they came. This single certainty sets in motion the long series of word games played mostly by Guil and Ros in act 1 and by Guil, Ros, and the Player in act 2, culminating in the frenetic activity of act 3. Throughout the play Shakespeare's principal characters—Hamlet, Claudius, Gertrude, Polonius, Horatio, and Fortinbras—function peripherally as context for the central roles of Guil and Ros (protagonists) and the Player and his tragedians (antagonists).

By means of the verbal and physical games, the very reality of Ros and Guil's existence is questioned, thickening the texture of the play with Pirandellian games of illusion and reality. Role playing as reality takes over in the Player's talk of never having to change into costume because of never changing out of it. Accepting the Player's challenge to act out their roles rather than be mere spectators, Ros and Guil become the new spectator-hero, like Lord Malquist. In choosing, they acquire a significance heretofore lacking in their lives.

Some of the comments of the Player bear striking resemblance to those in Pirandello's *Henry IV*. At one point, the Player bursts out to Guil: "You don't understand the humiliation of it—to be tricked out of the single assumption which makes our existence viable—that somebody is watching . . ." (63). And he continues: "We're actors. . . . We pledged our identities, secure in the conventions of our trade that someone would be watching. And then, gradually, no one was. . . . No one came forward. No one shouted at us. The silence was unbreakable, it imposed itself upon us; it was obscene. We took off our crowns and swords and cloth of gold and moved silent on the road to Elsinore" (64).

Without his costume and audience, the Player resembles Henry IV, who explains his madness to the world as the single assumption that makes existence viable: "We're all fixed in good faith in a certain concept of ourselves. However, Monsignor, while you keep yourself in order, holding on with both your hands to your holy habit, there slips down from your sleeves, there peels off from you like . . . like a serpent . . . something you don't notice: life, Monsignor!"[7]

Later, to one of his counselors who, by Henry's bidding, is acting out a historical role, Henry utters sentiments that might well be those of Ros and Guil, and, even more explicitly, those of George

Moore in *Jumpers:* "Do you know what it means to find yourselves face to face with a madman—with one who shakes the foundations of all you have built up in yourselves, your logic, the logic of all your constructions?"[8]

Throughout their Beckettian word games, Stoppard's Eliotic main characters act out Pirandellian contradictory truths of reality and appearance, sanity and insanity, relativity and absoluteness.

When the play opened in New York in October 1967, its reviews echoed those in the British press earlier that year. To Clive Barnes it is "very funny, very brilliant, very chilling; it has the dust of thought about it and the particles glitter excitingly in the theatrical air."[9] Martin Gottfried described Stoppard's "clear-minded understanding of *Hamlet*" as "awesome and his use of the few Rosencrantz and Guildenstern scenes from the play" as "marvellously merged with his inventions for them." In Gottfried's description of the play as "terribly bright," "very literate, occasionally moving and very eclectic," there was also a reservation that has been frequently expressed about Stoppard's play of ideas, that "it hammers at a philosophical point of view that is never developed beyond the basic statement. Its existentialism is shallow and its debt to Samuel Beckett extreme. Mr. Stoppard is clever but his play is not profound. . . ."[10]

Perhaps C. W. E. Bigsby's view of *Rosencrantz and Guildenstern Are Dead* is a judgment that most accurately describes this first major drama by Stoppard: "While it is true that the argument behind *Rosencrantz and Guildenstern Are Dead* is not complex, its strength lies precisely in the skill with which he has blended humour with metaphysical enquiry, the success with which he has made the play's theatricality an essential element of its thematic concern. It is, indeed, a kind of *Waiting for Godot,* in which Vladimir and Estragon become university wits."[11]

Chapter Seven
Jumpers: This Turbulent Priest

"An Ex-Pharmacologist is Archbishop of York,"[1] reads the headline of an article in the *New York Times* of 5 July 1983. The article goes on to explain that Archbishop Habgood had studied science at Cambridge University, worked as a pharmacologist for five years and wrote books on the relationship between science and the church. Although disagreeing with the antinuclear minority in the Church of England, the archbishop admits to being frightened by the possible use of nuclear weapons should hostilities break out. On this divisive issue, however, he maintains that discussion should proceed slowly. He also supports the ordination of women into the priesthood.

Archbishop Habgood, indeed his very name, might well come right out of the fertile imagination of dramatist Stoppard. In *Jumpers*, produced at the National Theatre at the Old Vic in 1972, eleven years prior to the appointment of Archbishop Habgood, there is a character, Samuel Clegthorpe, an ex-veterinarian and a spokesman for agriculture, who has just been named archbishop of Canterbury. Along with University Vice-Chancellor Sir Archibald Jumpers and Logic Professor Duncan McFee, Clegthorpe is a philosophical gymnast, whose system of logical positivism Professor of Moral Philosophy George Moore prepares to debate.

Throughout the two acts of the play, two separate actions are taking place. In his study, George is rehearsing his upcoming debate in a competition for the chair of logic at a university. Immersed in the abstractions of proving the existence of God and the centuries-old beliefs in the absoluteness of good and evil, he is oblivious to the noisy activities occurring in his living room. Those activities include a secretary swinging on a trapeze and performing a striptease as she swings, a group of acrobats who construct a pyramid, a murder of one of the gymnasts by a shot (presumably by Dotty, George's wife, but not absolutely established), a television airing of two lunanauts quarreling on the moon, and, last but not least, the abortive attempts of his wife, a former popular singer, to sing a confused mixture of moon songs. All the activities from which George is totally detached are a part of a celebration of a political victory by a radical-liberal group.

The two lines of action—George's debate rehearsal and the mysterious murder of one of the jumpers at the party—merge at points in the play such as the scenes in which Dotty unsuccessfully attempts to engage the attention of George and those in which George fails to demonstrate his traditional theories on "good, bad and indifferent" while his antagonists, the relativists, successfully dispose of the murder victim and rationalize away the very idea of a crime. Although Stoppard's obvious sympathies are with the ineffectual absolutism of George, his fascination with the intellectual disputation of those absolutes is equally obvious.

The play develops into one long, brilliant debate about good and evil between the traditional philosophers and the relativists of modern logical positivism. The leading protagonist of the former is George Moore through whom Stoppard parodies the philosophical system of G. E. Moore, a real-life philosopher. In fact, George is sometimes mistaken by the uninformed as the author of G. E. Moore's work *Principia Ethica*. The premise for Stoppard's plot is the unfashionability of the chair of moral philosophy that George occupies, an inferior status owing in large part to his adherence to the old-fashioned absolutes of the dead philosopher whose name he bears. His competitor for the prestigious chair of logic is Duncan McFee, a philosophical relativist.

The parody of G. E. Moore in the character of George is doubled by Stoppard's use of another real-life philosopher, Sir Alfred Ayer, Wyckham Professor of Logic at Oxford University. Ayer is dramatized in the person of Sir Archibald Jumpers, vice-chancellor of Moore's university. As a pragmatic and relativistic philosopher, he is George's antagonist in Stoppard's brilliant high comedy of ideas. At one point, George considers publishing a collection of essays entitled *Language, Truth and God,* a parody of the title of Ayer's famous book on logical positivism, *Language, Truth and Logic.*

A third character stolen from real life is Dotty Moore, George's wife and a prematurely retired songstress, who carries the same name as her real-life counterpart. Ayer, who wrote a review of the play in the *Sunday Times* entitled "Love Among the Logical Positivists," asserts that the real singer "could have little objection to the purloining of her name," since she is so "enchantingly portrayed by Diana Rigg."[2]

It is these three characters around whom tumble the bizarre events that Stoppard with inspired lunacy weds to the philosophical debate between the traditionalists and the relativists.

As Dotty watches the gymnasts, she is disillusioned because their acts, which are supposed to be incredible, are only too credible. Indeed, she asserts that she can not only sing better but also jump higher than they. Her disillusionment finds expression in her attempt to sing a confused medley of moon songs, bits of "Shine On, Harvest Moon," "Blue Moon," and "Allegheny Moon." Overwhelmed by the credibility of the gymnasts, she (apparently) fires a shot, the pyramid collapses, and the voice of Archie (her lover) announces, "The party is over."

Stoppard notes in the play that what appears to be Dotty's drunkenness is actually her mental breakup. During the party, a television program transmits pictures of a moon landing by two British astronauts, Oates and Scott, one of whom must leave the other behind in order to return safely to earth. The space quarrel compounds the breaking up of her romantic world, a breakup that corresponds to the failure of her husband's philosophical position. Under the stress of his own problems, George remains unaware of his wife's condition or of the murder of the gymnast until the end of the play.

Act 1 consists of large blocks of George's rehearsed argument, dictated to his secretary, while the party activities and their aftermath transpire. Inspector Bones appears in response to George's complaint about the noise and, also, to another call about a murder. The act concludes with the reappearance of the gymnasts with a plastic bag into which the dead body (which turns out to be that of George's rival at the academic competition, Duncan McFee) is tied and carried away.

Like Malquist of Stoppard's novel, George attempts to deal with the moral, political, scientific, and personal chaos of his life by withdrawing from the events around him and then by reverting to earlier times for his own creation of order. His is a brilliantly confusing synthesis of the traditional propositions of philosophy, particularly on the nature of existence and the ethical questions of good and evil.

From Plato there are references to the "fire at the mouth of our cave" as George questions why his socks exist. "Because a sock maker made it, in one sense; because, in another, at some point previously, the conception of a sock arrived in the human brain; to keep my foot warm in a third, to make a profit in the fourth. There is reason and there is cause and there is the question, who made the sock-maker's maker? etcetera, very well, next! see, see, I move my foot which moves my sock . . . all move around the room, which moves round the sun, which also moves, as Aristotle said, though not round the earth. . . . There is reason and there is cause. . . ."[3] Causality is the link among actions, as Aquinas, Zeno, Bertrand Russell and his theory of descriptions, and others join Plato and Aristotle in George's philosophical romp through time.

At one point George shoots his arrow in demonstration of a theory of Zeno's, that "though an arrow is always approaching its target, it never quite gets there . . ." (28). Not until the end of the play does he realize that his rabbit Thumper has been hit by that arrow. Near the end of his dictation George denounces McFee, his archrival, for stripping both morality and aesthetics of their absoluteness and for reducing actions to their usefulness.

Throughout the rehearsal of his lecture, George appears unaware of his wife's emotional needs. At one point in her despondency, she asks him, "Haven't you invented God *yet?*" George replies,"Nearly; I'm having him typed out" (34). When she quotes Archie, George becomes angry and goes to the bathroom to shave. In response to his comment that the water in the goldfish bowl needs changing, Dotty takes the bowl to the bathroom, empties it and returns with the bowl on her head, looking like a moon astronaut in a bubble.

From Dotty, George finds out that the spokesman for agriculture, Samuel Clegthorpe, has been appointed archbishop of Canterbury. George is incredulous. At times, Dotty proves herself an intelligent debater as she argues intuitively with George's absolutes: "Things do not *seem,* on the one hand, they *are:* and on the other hand, bad is not what they can *be.* . . . But good and bad, better and worse, these are not real properties of things, they are just expressions of our feelings about them" (41).

Her feelings today, she says, are not good. She decides not to see Archie today, if George so wishes. "It'll be just you and me under that old-fashioned, silvery harvest moon, occasionally blue, jumped over by cows and completed by Junes, invariably shining on the one I love; well known in Carolina, much loved in Allegheny, familiar in

Vermont; . . . *Keats's* bloody moon!—for what has made the sage or poet write but the fair paradise of nature's light—And *Milton's* bloody moon! rising in clouded majesty, at length apparent queen unveiled her peerless light and oe'r the dark her silver mantle threw—And Shelley's sodding maiden with white fire laden, whom mortals call the— *(weeping) Oh yes, things were in place then!"* (41). The disintegrating emotional world of Dotty parallels George's philosophical breakdown in the play. Chaos replaces order.

Stoppard's sense of the bizarre is illustrated in the arrival of Inspector Bones and in the masterpiece of quid pro quo confusion that ensues. For George does not yet know of McFee's murder, yet the inspector assumes he does. They converse on a mutually incorrect assumption. And adding to the farcical interplay of the practical and the philosophical, when Inspector Bones arrives, flowers in hand for his songstress-idol, he is met by George with shaving cream on his face and a bow and arrow in his hand. The farce is heightened by Bones's cognomen syndrome as he addresses George with a variety of names: Sidney, Clarence, Wilfred, etc.

The last scene of act 1 is performed in mime. Bones has gone into the bedroom to investigate the murder. Jumpers in their yellow suits move in to remove the body, as, to the music of "Sentimental Journey," Archie, "like a magician about to demonstrate a trick" (56), unfolds a large plastic bag in which the body is put. On the last beat of the song only Dotty and Archie remain on stage.

Act 2 continues the murder investigation by Inspector Bones. When Archie reappears, as psychiatrist to Dotty, Bones reads from Archie's calling card: "Sir Archibald Jumper, M.D., D.Phil., D.Litt., L.D., D.P.M., D.P.T. *(Gym)*. . . . What's all that?" (61). In his role as a pragmatist and philosophical jumper, Archie replies: "I'm a doctor of medicine, philosophy, literature and law, with diplomas in psychological medicine and P.T. including gym" (61). He is all of these, in addition to being vice-chancellor of Professor Moore's university, as Bones discovers. Stoppard's punning on Archie's title and, indeed, the multiple identity given Archie are but some of the means by which he is caricatured as opposed to the sympathetically satirized characterization of George.

Under the pretext of dermatological examinations, Archie is found in Dotty's bed. Asked by George what he is doing there, he replies: "Therapy takes many forms." "You examine her?" questions George.

"Oh yes, I like to keep my hand in. You must understand, my dear Moore, that when I'm examining Dorothy I'm not a lawyer or a philosopher. Or a gymnast, of course" (70).

In a manic pace of events, Archie informs Bones that McFee's body has been found in a bag in a park and that he himself had conducted the autopsy. Adding to the lunacy of things, Bones, accused of raping Dotty, has disappeared.

When Crouch, the porter, arrives, he provides pieces of missing information. As it turns out, when George's rival, McFee, would come around to wait for George's secretary, with whom he was conducting an affair, Crouch would engage McFee in philosophical discussions, thereby becoming quite a student of philosophy. He undergoes a dillusionment similar to that of Dotty and George. Crouch reports that, disturbed by the quarrel between the moon astronauts and by a similar situation in which actual Antarctic explorers, also named Oates and Scott, found themselves, McFee admitted that he had "seen the future . . . and it's yellow" (80). The color of the physical gymnasts' suits is yellow, like that assigned by Stoppard to the philosophical gymnastics of the relativists.

In the final scene of the play, Geroge discovers the impaled Thumper on top of the closet door; as he steps down, there is a crunch, and Pat, the tortoise is also dead. George's goldfish has already died, and George cries: "Dotty! Help! Murder!" as he falls to the floor. The proofs of his philosophical position have collapsed.

The play does not end with the second act but with a surrealistic "coda." George's cry for help is amplified and continued in a dreamlike enactment of the academic debate. In the dream, Crouch conducts the symposium and calls on Archie, Clegthorpe, and Dotty to speak. Archie's short speech receives shattering applause. As yellow-clothed ushers flip into the middle of the stage, Clegthorpe "flips" philosophically. Like Becket of Henry II fame, who chose church over state, Clegthorpe renounces jumperism in favor of orthodoxy.

The debate turns into a court trial, and Archie asks no more questions of Clegthorpe. He attempts, rather, to divert him by picking up the archbishop's reference to Lambeth, his residence in London. Substituting *Holborn* for *Lambeth,* Archie quotes directly from *Richard III* (act 3, scene 4): "My Lord Archbishop, when I was last in Lambeth I saw good strawberries in your garden—I do beseech you send for some" (85).

Archie's frustration with the lapsed archbishop is expressed in another familiar rehetorical question that recalls the Becket-Henry II quarrel: "Will no one rid me of this turbulent priest!" (85). Then, like the shot fired into the pyramid of acrobats at the beginning of the play, another rings out. This time it is Clegthorpe who is knocked out of the pyramid, as was McFee earlier. In a bravura speech of futility, George concludes with a list of witnesses to his philosophical argument, all of them dead, including "the late Herr Thumper." Confusing Zeno Evil, St. Thomas Augustine, and Jesus Moore, he demonstrates total disintegration, as Dotty sings the final words without music: "Goodbye spoony Juney Moon."

Combining courtroom, gymnasium, music hall, and university debating hall into one, Stoppard fuses "merely physical" and "metaphysical" (Dotty's terms) in this ending to his comic vision of contemporary ethical gymnastics. Although George Moore has failed to turn time back forty years (when things went off track), he is portrayed as the sympathetic side of the debate. The philosophical gymnasts—Archie, McFee, and Clegthorpe—with their relativistic, intuitional, pragmatic ethics (which include the explaining away of a murder) contrast sharply with George's failed philosophy but decent behavior.

Unlike its predecessor, *Rosencrantz and Guildenstern Are Dead,* and its successor, *Travesties, Jumpers* does not derive from another play nor parody another author's play. It does, however, parody real characters: G. E. Moore, Sir Alfred Ayer, and Dorothy Moore.

Stoppard told Tynan that "he had been reading the logical positivists with fascinated revulsion." Since he could not accept their views, "he was toying with the idea of a play whose entire second act would be a lecture in support of moral philosophy."[4] In December 1970, Stoppard met with Tynan, Laurence Olivier, and John Dexter at Tynan's house in Kensington in an abortive reading of a rough draft of the play, and "it took all the backslapping of which Dexter and I were capable to persuade him (Stoppard) that the play was worth saving."[5] Two years after the conversation between Tynan and Stoppard, the play opened at the Old Vic to the approbation of audiences and critics, and, of course, to the delight of academics, who enjoyed the intellectual debates.

One of Stoppard's strongest admirers, Professor Ayer, parodied in the play, reviewed it favorably and, indeed, claimed that "Tom is the only living dramatist whose work I would go to see just because he wrote it."[6]

If the play has a theme, it consists, as Ayer has written, of an argument "between those who believe in absolute values for which they seek a religious sanction, and those more frequently to be found among contemporary philosophers, who are subjectivists or relativists in morals, utilitarians in politics, and atheists or at least agnostics." If the play has a moral, it is that "George was humane, and therefore human, in a way the others were not."[7] Taking issue with Stoppard's handling of the positivists, Ayer concludes his review with the comment that even logical positivists are capable of love.

The chaos caused by modern events such as moon landings and moral relativists is a familiar Stoppardian theme going back to his novel, in which Moon is destroyed and Malquist creates his own eighteenth-century context. George Moore attempts to be a Boot character, but ends as a Moon, a victim of himself and his times.

In the tradition of *Rosencrantz and Guildenstern Are Dead,* which Stoppard developed from an earlier short play, *Jumpers,* too, has a preexistence in his television drama *Another Moon Called Earth.* In this play, a married couple, Penelope and Bone, are experiencing deteriorated personal relations, like those of George and Dotty. A moon landing here as in *Jumpers* has its impact on Penelope, and she takes to her bed, as does Dotty. Bone is writing a book, as George attempts to write his lecture, both concerned with the causality and connections in events. Penelope's nurse dies mysteriously, as does Duncan McFee, and Penelope, like Dotty, takes a lover, although it is not certain that he is her lover.

Both *Jumpers* and *Another Moon Called Earth* draw on situations and characters from *Lord Malquist and Mr. Moon.* In that novel both Malquist and Moon attempt to write, there is a murder, and Jane and in a lesser sense, Laura, undergo personal upheavals similar to Dotty's and Penelope's. The public event in the novel is not a moon landing (the beginning of a new era) but the funeral of the last great hero (the end of an old order). While the females in all three works disintegrate emotionally, the males face moral or intellectual chaos.

With the brilliant acting of Diana Rigg and Michael Hordern in the London production and the fluid staging of a deliberately chaotic plot, *Jumpers* opened to favorable reviews. In New York, however, critics were tentative and mixed in their reviews of the American production of *Jumpers.* The cumbersome staging and the performances by

Brian Bedford and Jill Clayburgh suffered much by comparison with their London predecessors. In spite of distractions, however, the play itself was applauded for its "verbal and intellectual wizardry."[8] Stoppard was hailed, as one writer put it, as perhaps "unequaled in today's English-speaking theater" in his wit, his "zany theatrical invention with cerebration," and his possession of a value that "shines, even through a glass darkly."[9] "At its best *Jumpers* suggests the Shaw of *Man and Superman,* the Wilder of *The Skin of Our Teeth,*"[10] wrote the *Time* critic. And Barnes "cannot really think of any English writer since John Donne who has been able to joke in such amusing philosophical terms. Mr. Stoppard is not a philosopher—he is very definitely a playwright. But he uses the world and that world's thought that he finds around him in something of the wild, dizzy and exhilarating manner of a metaphysical poet."[11]

Chapter Eight
Travesties: Caviar to the General Public

Stoppard's fourth full-length stage play and the third in the trilogy of major dramas that have taken the theater world by storm is *Travesties,* a play for which he read voluminously on Lenin, James Joyce, and dadaist art. To bring Lenin, Joyce, and the dadaist Tristan Tzara, to life on stage, Stoppard creates a fictional situation in Zurich during a time when all three men were living there. The historical possibility of the meeting of three revolutionary figures in politics, fiction, and art is joined with an actual happening in the theater in 1918, when Joyce was the business manager of the English Players, whose first production was Oscar Wilde's *The Importance of Being Earnest.* The means by which the historical and theatrical events are joined is an insignificant character, Henry Carr, through whose consciousness the history-making revolutionary events are filtered. Henry Carr, a minor British consulate official in Zurich in 1918, had played the role of Algernon for Joyce's company, and now as an old man with scattered memories he reenacts the events of those momentous days.

The major characters in the play represent the revolutions converging in Zurich during a time when the new world (post–World War I) was being born. In literature, James Joyce was writing the new era's major novel, *Ulysses.* In art, the dadaists, represented by Tristan Tzara, a minor artist of that group, were advocating chance as the determinant in life and art. In politics, there was Lenin who in Stoppard's play uses the occasion to advocate his theory of art as a force for social change. These three vastly different characters debate divergent views on the nature and purpose of art. In *Travesties,* however, unlike *Jumpers,* the debate of ideas is handmaiden to the brilliantly inventive parodies of the styles of Joyce, Tzara, and Lenin. The parodies themselves, rather than the intellectual exchanges, constitute the debate.

For Joyce art is its own excuse for being, and he is obviously Stoppard's *raisonneur*. For Tzara art, like historical events, is a matter of chance; indeed, chance is the very design of art, a theory Tzara demonstrates by tearing up the words of a Shakespearean sonnet and rearranging them into a nonsense poem. For Lenin art and society are closely linked, the former as an instrument of change for the latter. Obviously Lenin is not Stoppard's spokesman, as is clearly dramatized by Stoppard through the person of Brodie in a much later play, *The Real Thing* (1982).

Although these three major characters provide the thematic coherence in the play, they themselves are structurally unified by a plot in which two other real-life characters, A. Percy Bennett and Henry Carr, consulate employees in Zurich at the time, are dramatized. Like Rosencrantz and Guildenstern in the earlier play, Bennett and Carr, peripheral in real life, take center stage here (particularly Carr). It is through Carr's erratic memory that major historical events are revealed.

Using the play-within-a-play metaphor, as in *Rosencrantz and Guildenstern Are Dead,* Stoppard brings together the history-making events through the personal lives of some of the minor fictional characters— Gwen, Joyce's devoted secretary, and Cecily, a devout Leninist who happens to be the librarian. Both women, although loyal to their idols, fall in love, Gwen with Tzara and Cecily with Carr. In twists of mistaken identity Tzara and Carr find themselves reenacting situations analogous to those of Jack/Ernest Worthing and Algernon in Wilde's play. The two women, whose names are taken directly from Wilde's play, mistakenly swap their respective employers' manuscripts, much like the situation of the handbag in *The Importance of Being Earnest.* Within this highly improbable wedding of history and art, Stoppard creates some of the most dazzling debates in all his plays, this time on the nature and relationship of politics and art.

Once again, as in the two earlier major plays, the one derived from Shakespeare and influenced by Beckett and the other with its sources in the moral-philosophical arguments of George Moore and Professor A. J. Ayer, *Travesties* is derivative. The stodgy prose of Lenin, the exuberant Joycean language, and the Wildean farcical situations and wit are all immediately recognizable to those familiar with these famous figures. Indeed, *Travesties* is something of an elitist play for those acquainted with the political, literary, and artistic revolutions of the twentieth century.

The imaginative leaps that Stoppard makes possible by means of the erratic memory of Henry Carr, both a reliable and an unreliable narrator, are daringly successful. The dazzling language written for the actor, John Wood, is sheer magic. Michael Billington describes it as a "pyrotechnical feat that combines Wildean pastiche, political history, artistic debate, spoof-reiminiscence, and song-and-dance in marvelously judicious proportion. It radiates sheer intellectual *joie de vivre*. Exuberant and freewheeling!"[1]

As with *Jumpers, Travesties* is written in two acts. The scenes alternate between the drawing room of Carr's apartment and the Zurich Public Library. Act 1 opens with a library scene in which the audience is introduced immediately to the three historical figures of Joyce, Tzara, and Lenin and to the fictional librarian, Cecily, and secretary, Gwen. Cecily is attempting to quiet Tzara as he reads aloud a nonsense poem he has assembled from pieces of another poem that he had cut up and put into a hat. Joyce dictates to Gwen in familiar Joycean language. Sitting nearby, Lenin writes quietly, when his wife, Nadya, enters, and they begin conversing about the Russian revolution that has begun.

The three styles of discourse—dadaist, Joycean, and the somberly Leninist—with their sharply contrasting natures are, at the very outset of the play, the beginning of what develops into the most intoxicating reinvention of language on the modern English stage. Indeed, the theft of Wilde's plot, the fictionalizing of the meeting of the three revolutionaries, and the expected Stoppardian debate of ideas seem but a structural excuse for the luxurious indulgence in language for its own sake, an indulgence that only increases in speed, color, and intensity as the action progresses.

It is in the next scene, in Carr's apartment, that Stoppard's "central intelligence" appears in the person of Carr, a minor consular bureaucrat. It is through his reminiscences that the audience relives the revolutionary events of the time and that Stoppard conducts his parodic orchestration of language and ideas.

In a five-page monologue, Carr remembers his acting days and his many associations with Joyce. He calls his memories "Life and times, friend of the famous," a title that evokes one of Stoppard's short stories: "Life, Times: A Fragment." Carr has difficulty remembering the name of Algernon, the role he had played in Joyce's production of Wilde's play. He has equal difficulty remembering Joyce's name because it is feminine. A favorite joke of Stoppard's in many of his plays is the cognomen syndrome, and Carr suffers from the weakness. He is able to remember only that Joyce's name is feminine and addresses him variously as Doris, Phyllis, and Janice. His difficulty continues throughout the play and creates both comedy and the questioning of the reliability of the narrator.

But Carr does remember very clearly many details about the facts surrounding the activities of the three revolutionaries. He remembers that Spiegelgasse was the street of the revolutions, that Lenin was a tenant on that street, and that Tzara frequented the Meierei Bar there, the crucible of antiart and the cradle of dada. As he reminisces, Bennett, his manservant, enters and in reply to Carr's question about the news in the newspapers and telegrams that are put on the sideboard, Bennett proceeds to give Carr not only the news, but his attitudes about the news.

Carr's earlier monologue now shifts into a dialogue between the two men, an interesting one, since in real life Bennett had been Carr's superior at the British consulate in Zurich. Stoppard switches the relationship here, probably to emphasize, by means of the keen knowledge and intelligence of Bennett, the indifference of Carr to the events swirling about them. Bennett's comments are wide-ranging, from the political events exploding in Russia to the revolutions occurring in the art world.

The use of Carr's unreliable memory as a filtering consciousness for the world-shaking events of the time allows Stoppard the freedom he needs to shift back and forth between the present and the past and to preserve the ambiguity necessary to Stoppard's fictionalizing actual events into an imaginary situation. As Carr fragmentarily remembers events, they become the stuff of Stoppard's drama.

He remembers Tzara's arrival at the apartment to ask for the hand of his sister, Gwen, at the same time that Joyce and Gwen arrive to discuss with Carr the financial arrangements for Carr's role in a play Joyce is directing, Wilde's *The Importance of Being Earnest*.

At this meeting, Stoppard begins his famous parodies of dadaist art and Joycean language, as Tzara and Joyce exchange attitudes on art. In his habitual financial straits, Joyce asks Carr, then Tzara, and, finally, Bennett for the loan of a pound. As Tzara vanishes with Gwen, Joyce concludes the scene with a limerick about Tzara, Robert Burns, and himself:

> A Rumanian rhymer I met
> used a system he based on roulette

> His reliance on chance
> was a def'nite advance
> and yet . . . and yet . . . and yet. . . .
>   . . .
> When I want to leave things in the air
> I say, "Excuse me, I've got to repair
> to my book about Bloom—"[2]

The next scene involves Tzara and Carr in a debate, both characters "straight out of *The Importance of Being Earnest*" (36). Tzara's main contention is that "causality is no longer fashionable owing to the war" (36) and that "clever people try to impose a design on the world and when it goes calamitously wrong they call it fate. In point of fact, everything is Chance, including design" (37). Carr's response that "it is the duty of the artist to beautify existence" rather than to "jeer and howl and belch at the delusion that infinite generations of real effects can be inferred from the gross expression of apparent cause" evokes from Tzara four lines of chanted "dada" (37). Carr insists on conventional values of words like "*patriotism, duty, love, freedom,* king and country, brave little Belgium, saucy little Serbia" (39), while Tzara argues the corruption of music and language as "traditional sophistries for waging wars of expansion and self-interest, presented to the people in the guise of rational argument set to patriotic hymns . . ." (39). The argument winds down to Tzara's chanting the word "da-da" as Carr chants "we're here because we're here . . . because we're here. . ." (40).

As the two men get on with the business of Tzara's visit—his request for the hand of Carr's sister, Gwendolyn—the subject turns to Joyce, Lenin, and Cecily. Tzara explains his signing the name Jack on his library card in order to impress Cecily, who has no time for the dadaists and who knows of Tzara's contempt for bourgeois art. Tristan, he had informed her, is his younger bohemian brother. This deception creates the confusion that resembles the plot of Wilde's play.

To ingratiate himself with Gwen, whose admiration for Joyce is unqualified, Tzara, attempting to establish his commonality with Joyce as a poet, informs the latter:

> For your masterpiece
> I have great expectorations
> (Gwen's squeak, "Oh")

> For you I would eructate a monument.
> (Oh)
> art for art's sake—I defecate.
>
> (48)

And Joyce replies with a recitation of his parody of the ballad of Mr. Dooley, including a statement about his frequently criticized neutrality in World War I:

> Who is the meek philosopher who doesn't care a damn
> About the yellow peril or the problem of Siam
> And disbelieves that British Tar is water from life's fount
> And will not gulp the gospel of the German on the mount.
>
> (50)

After Joyce and Carr talk over the arrangements for Carr's role in the play, the two retire to the next room so that Carr can see a copy of *The Importance of Being Earnest*. Left in the room, Gwen and Tzara discuss his poetic techniques by means of Gwen's quoting Shakespeare's eighteenth sonnet and Tzara's cutting the sonnet into its words, putting the pieces into a hat and randomly picking them out and rearranging the words in dadaist style. To her they are but whirling words. Gwen expresses her dismay in lines from *As You Like It:* "Truly I wish the gods had made thee poetical" (54). Joyce reenters the room as Tzara and Gwen embrace.

When Gwen leaves the room to tell her brother Henry the news of Tzara's proposal, Joyce begins a long dialogue with Tzara in the style of the Ithaca section of *Ulysses,* in which Stephen Dedalus and Leopold Bloom engage in a question-and-answer session after their adventure in Nighttown. The questions Joyce puts to Tzara involve the nature and history of dadaist art. The parodic style includes even a reference to urinating, as in the *Ulysses* scene. As the ego of Tzara manifests itself in his assertion that "making poetry should be as natural as making water—" (62), their irreconcilable differences on the nature of art emerge. Tzara's artistic technique is to smash existing forms and traditional subject matter. Joyce's definition of the artist is that of one who illuminates and is "put among men to gratify—capriciously—their urge for immortality. . . . If there is any meaning in any . . . [of history], it is in what survives as art, yes even in the celebration of tyrants, yes even in the celebration of nonentities" (62). It is the broken pots of history, "enriched, by a tale of heroes . . .

above all, of Ulysses, the wanderer, the most human, the most complete of all heroes—husband, father, son, lover, farmer, soldier, pacifist, politician, inventor and adventurer . . . yes by God *there's* a corpse that will dance for some time yet and *leave the world precisely as it finds it . . .*" (62–63).

Earlier in this scene, Joyce had put on the hat with the bits of paper Tzara had put into it, looking foolish with paper clinging to his head and clothes. But when Tzara uses the word "conjure," Joyce pulls silk hankies from the hat, then flags, and, finally, a rabbit, illustrating his own definition of the artist, not as a man who changes the world, but who puts together the broken shards of history with his magic, as Homer had from the destructive war between Greece and Troy.

With the return to Carr's reminiscing, the audience is informed about the actual lawsuit and countersuit brought by Carr against Joyce and Joyce against Carr, the result of Joyce's refusal to pay for the suit Carr wore in the play and, in turn, Joyce's charge of slander.

Stoppard's magic, like Joyce's, is the containing of epic events of history and art within the context of the trivial, the trivial here consisting of a personal conflict over money between Joyce and Carr. This technique of trivialization, strikingly demonstrated in *Rosencrantz and Guildenstern Are Dead,* is underscored in Carr's reference to the outcome of the trial as a travesty of justice and in the partial revenge Carr gained on Joyce in a dream he had about twenty years later, in 1940, with Joyce returned to Switzerland at the outbreak of World War II. In the dream, Carr had Joyce "in the witness box, a masterly cross-examination, case practically won . . . and I *flung* at him—'And what did you do in the great War?' 'I wrote *Ulysses,*' he said. 'What did you do?' Bloody nerve" (65). Carr had been invalided from World War I, and his contempt for Joyce's neutrality and, consequently, for his literary achievement, *Ulysses,* is one of the many travesties in the play.

As in *Jumpers,* the debate of ideas constitutes most of act 1. Act 2, then, contains the actions that involve the clearing up of mistaken identities of Tristan and Carr and the return of switched briefcases to their rightful owners, Joyce and Lenin, in a close parody of the plot of *The Importance of Being Earnest.*

But before the resolution of the plot begins, there is a long lecture by Cecily on Leninist theories that she espouses. The lecture style has puzzled critics because of the change in tone from the imaginative language of the first act. It is straightforward and serious, in keeping with the prosaic style of Lenin, but out of keeping with the rest of the play. As a lecture on the revolutionary events of the time, it does serve as a counterpart of the history of dadaism provided by Tzara to Joyce in the first act. It also stylistically balances the long reminiscences of Carr early in act 1 and provides a means for the convergence of the ideas debate and the Wildean action of the play. Handled by a lesser artist, this pastiche of styles could easily fail. Stoppard's artistry, like Joyce's pulling rabbits out of a hat, does pull off the trick.

As Cecily lectures on the significance of the political events that are transpiring, her prologue is interrupted by the arrival of Carr (as Tristan) to pursue his romantic cause with her. She uses him as a means to continue her advocacy of Leninist principles. Carr, representing conventional English attitudes, argues that Marx had it all wrong. Calling him a Kant-struck prig, she accuses him of not attending to her arguments, but rather imagining how she would look stripped off to her knickers.

Lighting effects create a surrealistic cabaret scene in which Carr imagines her as a stripper. Cecily, equally carried away in her rhetorical flourish, jumps on her desk and reaches a verbal climax:

In England the rich own the poor and the men own the women. Five per cent of the people own eighty per cent of the property. The only way is the way of Marx, and of Lenin, the enemy of all revisionism—of economism—opportunism—liberalism—of bourgeois anarchist individualism—of quasi-socialist ad hoc-ism, of syndicalist quasi-Marxist populism—liberal quasi-communist opportunism, economist quasi-internationalist imperialism. . . . (78)

Her trancelike recitation matches Carr's erotic imagination and is cut off by his "Get 'em off!"

Lights snap on, and normalcy in the library resumes. Cecily informs Carr-cum-Tristan that ever since Jack (Tristan's assumed identity) had told her his younger brother Tristan was a decadent nihilist, it had been her girlish dream to reform and love him. The two embrace. The Wildean confusion of names develops farcically when the real Tristan (Jack, to Cecily) enters, and Cecily informs him that she has reformed his rakish brother.

The Lenins fade back into the picture as they discuss the plans for their return to Russia. Lights then center on Carr as he narrates his place in the revolutionary events in which he is swept up. As Cecily's admirer he had got "pretty close" to Lenin, "and I'd got a pretty good idea of his plans, in fact I might have stopped the whole Bolshevik thing in its tracks, but—here's the point. *I was uncertain.* What was the right thing? And then there were my feelings for Cecily. And don't forget, *he wasn't Lenin then!*" (81). Carr's role in the entire play is expressed in this comment. He functions in much the same way as Rosencrantz and Guildenstern in Stoppard's earlier play, a Moon character who thinks he understands or tries to understand, but ultimately cannot move events. Although as a character within the events he is uncertain, he is an insignificant figure who takes on significance by the author's manipulation of him as narrator.

In a succession of scenes, Carr and Tzara discuss history, the former insisting that Lenin must be stopped so that the moderately socialist Kerensky and his group could have power and the latter asserting that, do what one will, "to a Dadaist history comes out of a hat too" (83).

Lenin's long monologue follows in which ideas of history and art intersect. He claims that although writers may be free to say whatever they like, the party is also free to expel them if they advocate antiparty views. The comment is followed by another about absolute freedom as sheer hypocrisy even in a bourgeois democracy. There are the bourgeois publisher and the bourgeois public who make demands on the writer, whereas "socialist literature and art will be free because the idea of socialism and sympathy with the working people, instead of greed and careerism, will bring ever new forces to its ranks" (85). Lenin's preferences of Russian writers are mentioned, and to the music of Beethoven's *Appassionata Sonata,* the light goes out, and the Wildean play situation takes over.

Cecily and Gwen converse in limerick rhythms about their future friendship, their romantic interest in Tristan, and their current involvement in art and politics: Gwen's admiration for Joyce's poetry and Cecily's for Lenin's ideas. Their divergences are converging. Cecily in a reference to 16 June 1904 (the day on which the events of Joyce's *Ulysses* occur) admits that the reason for her call on Gwen is to remind her that "there's a fee due on Homer's *Odyssey* and the *Irish Times* for June 1904" (91). As their conversation moves to "Jack" and Tristan, the focus becomes Tristan, whom each claims as her man. At the appropriate moment in their confusion, Carr enters and is identified by Gwen as her brother. When Cecily finds out that he is not Tristan Tzara, the decadent nihilist, but the British consul,

Henry Carr, the two women replay lines from *The Importance of Being Earnest:*

> GWEN: A gross deception has been practised upon us. My poor wounded Cecily!
> CECILY: My sweet wronged Gwendolen! (94)

Bennett once more, refrain-style, announces to Carr that he has put the newspapers and telegrams on the sideboard, and Carr once more asks if there is anything of interest. He is informed of the favorable reviews his role as Algernon received from the critics, whereupon he unleashes epithets—Irish lout, Deirdre, Bridget, Joyce, Sponger—on Joyce for handing him a payment, a "tip," of ten francs for the performance.

Joyce enters in an agitated state over his being handed "an ill-tempered thesis purporting to prove, amongst other things, that Ramsay MacDonald is a bourgeois lickspittle gentleman's gentleman" (97), when, in fact, he had been looking for his chapter in *Ulysses* on the Homeric episode of the Oxen of the Sun, which Gwen had typed. The chapter had been confused in an earlier library scene with a manuscript of Lenin's. Tzara offers his contemptuous criticism of the Joycean chapter he had read, saying it had much in common with the mismatched clothing Joyce was wearing. Carr, lapsing into a parody of Joyce's style, asks: "And is it a chapter, inordinate in length and erratic in style, remotely connected with midwifery?" Joyce replies: "It is a chapter which by a miracle of compression, uses the gamut of English literature from Chaucer to Carlyle to describe events taking place in a lying-in hospital in Dublin" (97). Carr then triumphantly produces the other misplaced folder with Joyce's chapter. When Gwen and Cecily recognize the mistake, the confused identities of persons and folders are righted, and the two couples dance as do Joyce and Bennett.

The play concludes with Old Carr and Old Cecily discussing the past over a cup of tea, Cecily commenting that she never helped Lenin write *Imperialism, the Highest Stage of Capitalism,* and Carr recalling "Great days . . . Zurich during the war. Refugees, spies, exiles, painters, poets, writers, radicals of all kinds. I knew them all. Used to argue far into the night . . . at the Odeon, the Terrasse . . . I learned three things in Zurich during the war. I wrote them down. Firstly, you're either a revolutionary or you're not, and if you're not you might as well be an artist as anything else. Secondly, if you can't be an artist, you might as well be a revolutionary. . . . I forget the third thing" (98–99).

The characters of *Travesties* belong to the Moon-Malquist syndrome of Stoppardian characters. On the one hand, there is Henry Carr, who lives on the periphery of events and is helplessly insignificant. Caught up in the sweep of those events, he becomes the eyes through which the audience sees them. Just as Moon functions ineffectually on the day of Winston Churchill's funeral, as Ros and Guil obey the call of the court at Elsinore, and as Dotty Moore's romantic illusions are shattered by quarreling astronauts on the moon, so Henry Carr is ultimately eclipsed by events involving Lenin, James Joyce, and Tristan Tzara. On the other hand, there are the spectator-heroes who have withdrawn from the chaos with style: Lord Malquist, the Player and his tragedians, Joyce and Tzara, and, perhaps, George Moore, although in a much less emphatic manner.

The play is significant as Stoppard's purest illustration of his love of literary jokes, puns, stylistic parodies, derivational techniques, and in general an intoxication with his acquired language perhaps unrivaled in English literature except by Shakespeare and James Joyce.

The title itself concerns not only the prolific travesties of styles within this play but those in nearly everything Stoppard has written. *Enter a Free Man* as a parody of Arthur Miller has already been discussed. *Lord Malquist and Mr. Moon* in its labyrinthine winding through London streets on Churchill's funeral day parodies Leopold Bloom's famous journey through Dublin on that fateful 16 June 1904 in *Ulysses*. In addition, by direct references to Eliot's "The Love Song of J. Alfred Prufrock," Stoppard provides a double parodic layer in his novel. The ingenious adaptation of both Beckett and Shakespeare in *Rosencrantz and Guildenstern Are Dead* needs no further comment here. In *Travesties*, art—language for Stoppard—reaches its fullest justification in its brilliant parodies of Joycean, dadaist, Wildean, and Leninist language.

In the tradition of the best writers who have used history and literature as grist for their artistic mills—Shakespeare, Joyce, and Beckett—Stoppard practices the magic of pulling rabbits out of hats containing torn bits of paper. In this regard, *Travesties* is Stoppard's major achievement. *Rosencrantz and Guildenstern Are Dead* plays with philosophical matters of existence and destiny, *Jumpers* with a moral philosophy, but *Travesties* unabashedly celebrates the vehicle of the dramatist's art: language.

Even the fictional characters, Gwen and Cecily, and the petty bureaucrats, Carr and Bennett, are caught up in the celebration of words. And, although Lenin is concerned mostly with the Russian revolution, and although he adheres theoretically to the political function of art, even he admires prerevolutionary Russian writers and Beethoven's music. The celebration of life through art, the substance and style of Beckett's and Joyce's writing, is Stoppard's in his parodic romp through the writings and ideas of others.

The obvious theme in *Travesties* is the nature and purpose of art as these are debated in the persons of Joyce, Tzara, and Lenin. Joyce's theory is that art celebrates and even justifies history by re-creating from its shards "a corpse that will dance for some time yet and *leave the world precisely as it finds it* " (63). As dadaist, Tzara contends that existing forms must be smashed, and he argues that even what appears to artists to be design is merely chance. And, finally, Lenin insists on the importance of art as an instrument for social change. In a later play, *The Real Thing* (1982), Joyce's (and Stoppard's) view of art is forcefully dramatized in a fictional dramatist named Henry, as Lenin's theories are expressed through another fictional (but boorish) dramatist named Brodie.

If the debate about the nature and purpose of art forms the literal theme of *Travesties,* the theme would seem to be subsumed in the language through which it is communciated. That language keeps shooting off fireworks blazing with magical colors and patterns, calling attention to itself in seeming oblivion to its content.

In her study, Felicia Londré identifies a variety of language tricks in *Travesties* that could easily elude the casual theatergoer. In the opening library scene, for example, Tzara's assembly of a poem by picking words from a hat results in what seems a nonsense rhyme:

> Eel ate enormous appletzara
> key dairy chef's hat he'lllearn oomparah!
> Ill raced alas whispers kill later nut east,
> noon avuncular ill day Clara!
>
> (18)

To someone familiar with French, Londré points out, the poem could read:

> Il est énorme, s'appelle Tzara,
> Qui déréchef se hâte. Hilare non pareil!
> Il reste á la Suisse parcequ'il est un artiste.
> "Nous n'avons que l'art," il déclara![3]

And the English translation of the French reads:

> He is larger-than-life, is called Tzara,
> Who rushes headlong once again. Peerless jokester!
> He stays in Switzerland because he is an artist.
> "We have only art!" were his words.[4]

With Stoppard's by-now famous comment about his plays as ambushes for the audience, Londré's translation of dada into French and then into English, is indeed, a perceptive identification of a linguistic ambush. In addition, she calls attention to some of the many parodies, such as the use of "sense and consequence" as a play on Austen's *Sense and Sensibility* and the reference to the celebration of Joyce's *Ulysses* as "caviar for the general public," an inversion of the line from *Hamlet:* "The play, I remember, pleased not the million; 'twas caviar to the general."[5]

Not quite an ambush, since the English translation is provided, is the dialogue between Lenin and Nadya carried on in Russian and then spelled in phonetic English: "Da-da. Idiom damoi. On zhdyot. (Yes—yes. Come on home. He's waiting)" (20). The "Da-da" is a linguistic play on dadaism. The joke continues later when Tzara puns from the line of a popular song: "My heart belongs to dada." Even the dull Carr at one point reminisces about Tzara: "Tristan Tzara. Dada Dada Dada. Did he have a stutter?" (28).

It is, however, the audacious parodying of Joycean language throughout that upstages other parodies in *Travesties.* Near the beginning and at the end of Carr's long monologue in act 1, he talks about being "released into folds of snow-white feather beds, pacific civilian heaven! the mystical swissticality of it, the entente cordiality of it!, the Jesus Christ I'm out of it!—into the valley of the invalided—Carr of the Consulate!" (41). Imbedded in this line of Joycean word-formations is a reference to Tennyson's "The Charge of the Light Brigade."

Joyce's parody of the ballad of Mr. Dooley, the rhyming conversation between Gwen and Cecily, the Wildean inversions, the slipping from dialogue into music-hall songs, the various vaudevillian touches, the nonsense chanting of Tzara—all these reach their zenith in the parody of the Ithaca scene from *Ulysses*. By this means, Stoppard allows Tzara to provide a history of the dadaist movement as well as allowing Joyce to parody himself:

> JOYCE: What is the meaning of this?
>
> TZARA: It has no meaning. It is without meaning as nature is. It is Dada.
>
> . . .
>
> JOYCE: Are you the inventor of this sport or pastime?
>
> TZARA: I am not.
>
> JOYCE: What is the name of the inventor?
>
> TZARA: Arp.
>
> JOYCE: Is he your sworn enemy, pet aversion, bête noir, or otherwise persona non grata?
>
> TZARA: He is not.
>
> JOYCE: Is he your friend, comrade-in-arms, trusted confidant or otherwise pal, mate or crony?
>
> TZARA: He is. (56)

The catechism goes on for pages, as does Carr's monologue at the beginning and Lenin's near the end of the play.

It is at the end of the Ithaca parody that Tzara smashes whatever crockery is at hand, to demonstrate the necessity for demolishing the temple of art.

Joyce responds in a monologue on the nature of art: that whatever meaning is to be found in history is what art makes of it, "even in the celebration of tyrants, yes even in the celebration of nonenties" (62). The destruction of Troy is justified in the art of Homer (and consequently, of Joyce). The nonenties, one can assume, are the middle-class canvasser, Bloom, and the bureaucrat, Carr, justified in the art of Joyce and Stoppard respectively.

If *Travesties* thrives on parodies of other writers, it also derives from an earlier play of Stoppard's, *Artist Descending a Staircase*. In this radio play, the major public event is also World War I, and the three artists, like the three revolutionaries of *Travesties,* discuss respective art theories. The structure of time present and time past characterizes both plays. And dadaists function prominently, or at least are argued about, in both plays.

A major distinction of *Travesties* insofar as the plot mechanics are concerned is the absence of a death or a murder as part of the plot. The deaths of Rosencrantz and Guildenstern, Duncan McFee, theater critics, and others have become stock elements in both plot construction and parodic style in Stoppard's plays. The murder mystery element would be gratuitous, however, in *Travesties,* in which ambushes of language and stylistic tricks of various sorts replace the plot ambush.

The travesties of the title consist of brilliant trivializations of major events and major figures in those momentous events of the early twentieth century. As such, the characters of the play lack the total human dimensions found in the characters of *Rosencrantz and Guildenstern Are Dead* and, even more so, of *Jumpers.* In depicting Joyce, Tzara, and Lenin as fascinating travesties of themselves, Stoppard would seem to have created a dazzling self-travesty, perhaps the largest of all travesties in the play.

The play received notices that equaled the splendor of the play itself. Clive Barnes described the New York production in glowing terms, a "strange pas de quatre" from which Stoppard "has constructed a whole ballet of words, wit and oddly disturbing literary echoes."[6] T. E. Kalem described the play as a "tinderbox of a play blazing with wit, paradox, parody, and, yes, ideas. It is exhilaratingly, diabolically clever. The bloodline of Wilde and Shaw is not extinct while Tom Stoppard lives.[7]

Scholars, such as Richard Ellmann, whose book on Joyce Stoppard used as a source, have admired *Travesties.* Ellmann writes about "what might be called a stoppardism or a tomism, as when Tzara is accused of being 'Kant-struck,' and Wilde disparaged as 'coxcomb and bugbear of the Home Rule sodality.' These laundered obscenities perhaps convey some sense of the flagrant high spirits of this admirable play."[8] Ellmann's review, entitled "The Zealots of Zurich," puts academic approval on *Travesties,* as Ayer's "Love Among the Logical Positivists" does for *Jumpers.*

Chapter Nine
Night and Day:
Caliban at Charterhouse

Stoppard's fifth full-length stage play, *Night and Day* (1978), is a drama, rather than a comedy, of ideas. Like *Jumpers,* this drama is concerned with morality, but now the ethics involve not academic philosophers but practical journalists who find themselves in the middle of a potential African revolution. Unlike *Jumpers,* the style is naturalistic, rather than farcical and fantasy-ridden, the first play in this tradition since *Enter A Free Man.*

Night and Day is Stoppard's dramatic realization of a journalistic dream he once had: "to lie on the floor of an African airport while machine gun bullets zoomed over my typewriter."[1] Instead of an airport, however, Stoppard's location is the home of a copper mine owner, and instead of actual bullets in the opening scene, there is gunfire in the dream of a photographer, George Guthrie, who awakens from his nap to be confronted as an uninvited guest of the Carsons. But the bullets are real at the end when a young journalist, Jacob Milne, is killed in crossfire in hostile territory.

In his short stories and in *The Real Inspector Hound,* Stoppard had already drawn on his years in Bristol as a journalist and in London as theater critic for *Scene* magazine. In *Night and Day* journalists take center stage for the first time in a full-length drama that explores in depth ideas similar to those already debated by academics and artists in earlier plays.

In an interview with Ronald Hayman in 1976, Stoppard talked about wanting to write a play in a conventional vein, perhaps in the manner of Priestley or Rattigan. He was "sick of flashy mind-projections speaking in long, articulate, witty sentences about the great abstractions."[2] What he finally settled for in *Night and Day,* however, was not the "professor or a doctor with a grey-haired wife and problem child, and the maid comes in with the muffin dish and they talk about the weather a bit."[3] Instead, his variation of the formula involves a vastly different domestic arrangement: a British copper mine owner, his bored wife, and a precocious schoolboy son, living in an exotic fictional African country, Kambawe. The conventional English maid and muffins take the form of a native servant who serves alcoholic drinks to the visiting journalists. The large outline of a Priestley-Rattigan play is present, indeed, but converted from a domestic drama to the usual Stoppardian ideas debate between proponents of traditional, idealistic values and those of contemporary, pragmatic views.

Night and Day—the Cole Porter tune is played before curtain rise—follows the two-act structure of *Jumpers* and *Travesties*. Act 1 consists largely of intellectual debates and act 2 of fast-moving action that flows from the ideas set forth in the first half. Unlike the other two plays, however, events follow a chronological linear pattern. Emphasizing the conventional time sequence is Stoppard's use of a time-worn technique to climax the events: a secret, innocently revealed, on which the action of the drama turns. The secret consists of the revelation to Wagner by the young son, Allie, of the arrival at the Carsons of Mageeba, an Idi Amin–like dictator, for a meeting with the rebel leader, Shimbu. The information enables Wagner, although uninvited and unwelcome, to show up for that meeting in anticipation of a scoop and to forgo a journey with Guthrie to carry the message of the meeting to Shimbu. Consequently, Milne, the young journalist, takes Wagner's place on the mission.

The action of the play begins with the unannounced arrival of Richard Wagner and George Guthrie, a photographer-writer journalistic team, at the home of Ruth and Geoffrey Carson in Kambawe. They have been sent by the *Sunday Globe,* a weekly (evidently a variation of the *Sunday Times*), to cover the coming revolution. Later in the play it is revealed that the newspaper sent them to the Carson home on the tip by Milne that there was a telex to wire their stories home.

A free-lance journalist, Jacob Milne, is also here, having earlier scooped an interview with Shimbu for the *Globe*. His article, of course, was unfavorable to the English-educated Mageeba.

The first act develops the hostilities between Wagner and Milne, one a seasoned union journalist and the other an idealistic young reporter who is scornful in his independence of union membership with its restriction of press freedom, as he claims. To Wagner, Milne is the Grimsby scab who in the interest of a story is sometimes less than factual. He especially questions Milne's reporting "prose" rather than facts. To Milne, Wagner's abuse of him arises from an intolerance of principles different from his own. Milne especially resents the fact that the union would out of pique close down the newspaper in the last two-paper town of its size in the country.

In another ideas debate later in act 1, Ruth also engages Wagner in an articulate condemnation of the way the papers had handled her earlier marital difficulties. "The populace and the popular press. What a grubby symbiosis it is. Which came first? The rhinoceros or the rhinoceros bird?"[4] Later, engaging Milne in a similar denunciation of grubby journalism, she is told by him that tabloids are "the price you pay for the part that matters" (66).

Complicating her encounter with Wagner is Ruth's one-night sexual affair with him when she had been in London to make school arrangements for her son. She makes it clear to Wagner that she has no interest in him now and that she is attracted to the younger Milne.

The romantic and journalistic interests of the drama are catalyzed by the local political conflict, in which the financial interests of Geoffrey Carson loom large. For him the arranging of the secret meeting between Mageeba and Shimbu transcends all other matters, personal, moral, or philosophical. As a seasoned capitalist, he is cynical about the union journalist and detached from political causes or the needs of his wife. For Carson and Wagner, their professions come first. Carson's hard-headed realism is seen in his view of the impending conflict in Kambawe: "I think Shimbu wants the whole apple, and is using the time to get his supply line working. . . . I also think that the British and the Americans will protest, and all the time they're protesting the Russians will be interfering the stuffing out of Mageeba's army . . . and *that* the British and Americans will protest" (82–83).

The act ends with Milne appearing dressed like Action Man and angrily denounced by Guthrie, who prefers the seasoned Wagner as companion on the mission.

When Mageeba arrives, in act 2, as does the unwelcome Wagner, the debate on journalistic responsibility carried on earlier by Wagner, Milne, and Ruth is continued, only in a politically hostile situation. Mageeba is angry with the *Globe* for its unfavorable view of himself. A former student at the London School of Economics, he is an articulate antagonist to Wagner. In an attempt to assuage Mageeba's anger, Wagner flatters him by promising that his article will stress the dictator's anticommunist position. The response to Wagner's attempt at ingratiating himself with Mageeba is the latter's sudden striking of the journalist with his cane, knocking him to the floor.

The play ends swiftly as Guthrie excitedly arrives with the news of the abortive mission and of the death of Milne, who was killed as they neared their destination. Angry at the senseless death, he lashes out verbally at Mageeba. Mageeba turns around and walks out. Guthrie's honest outburst at the dictator is a strong contrast with the flattery of Wagner.

In spite of the highly serious and naturalistic language of the play, some of the usual Stoppardian irony and wit, although toned down, are in evidence. When Ruth, for instance, lies to her husband when he asks if she has met Wagner, she covers her lie by acknowledging him [Wagner] as "Mr. . . . Strauss . . . ?" When Wagner corrects her, carrying on her deception, she replies: "Wagner. Exactly. I knew it was Richard." And a Stoppardian pun is present in Ruth's refusal to call Wagner, Dick, since she is not terribly fond of the word. Wagner replies: "You could have fooled me" (39).

When Mageeba leaves, he takes a parting shot at Wagner and the *Globe*, as he comments: "Oh, one more thing, Mr. Wagner—would you make a note . . . it was not Othello I played at Charterhouse. It was Caliban. They always get it wrong" (102).

An unusual device in the play is Stoppard's use of the aside to express Ruth's unspoken thoughts. Employed by dramatists such as Eugene O'Neill in *Strange Interlude* and Harold Pinter in the distinctive pauses and silences of his plays, asides provide the audience with the contrast between what is said and what is really meant under the mask of language. On stage, Stoppard's asides are confusing, as it is difficult to distinguish between Ruth's spoken words and those that she is thinking. To the reader, however, the distinction is made by quotation marks around her thoughts. In O'Neill's plays, actors wear masks and drop them when they are thinking aloud or they step to the stage apron and address the audience. In Stoppard's play the verbal mask and its underlying truths run into each other indistinguishably.

Night and Day bears an especially interesting resemblance to Pinter's *The Homecoming* both in the situation of Ruth and, indeed, in her very name. Amid alien corn, both Ruths, in marital situations of boredom and uselessness, use sex as a means of engaging themselves meaningfully. Both feel ignored by their husbands and find or attempt to find some excitement with other men to meet their needs, in one case in the ancestral home of her husband and in the other in her own home. With Pinter's Ruth it is the two brothers and, possibly, the father, with whom Ruth becomes involved, and with Stoppard's Ruth it is the two journalists. Philosophy professor in one case and mine owner in the other, both husbands are so preoccupied with their professions that their wives' sexual and emotional needs must be met elsewhere.

Another similarity in the plays is the sudden, unexpected striking of Wagner by Mageeba. At moments of truth in Pinter's plays, *The Room* (1957) and *The Homecoming* (1965), Bert and Max fell their threatening usurpers to the floor.

A major coincidence of the play concerns its opening on 8 November 1978, one week before Pinter's *Betrayal*. Both plays were seen by critics as a literary betrayal of their authors' styles. Benedict Nightingale wrote that "no British playwright presently stands higher than either Harold Pinter or Tom Stoppard in the stockmarket of taste; and so it is natural that the coincidental opening of a play by each man within a week should have provoked avid comparisons among the culture brokers."[5]

Pinter's usual Kafka-like menaces and dislocations are replaced in *Betrayal* by a straightforward chronology of events, dramatized in reverse order. Similarly, the usual dadaist, bizarre events and language acrobatics of Stoppard's earlier dramas give way in *Night and Day* to conventional plot sequence and absence of visual and linguistic fireworks. Nightingale's surprise at the sudden turn of Pinter from his "talent of ambiguity" to a "drab triangle drama" and of Stoppard from his usual "fun philosophy" to slipping a "white collar over his usual motley"[6] echoed the response of most critics to both plays.

Notwithstanding this similarity in critical reception, Stoppard came out slightly ahead of Pinter in the comparisons of new dramas by England's most celebrated contemporary dramatists.

In their reviews, critics called attention to Evelyn Waugh's novel *Scoop* as an influence on Stoppard's play, although Stoppard's view of journalists is less cynical than Waugh's.

C. W. E. Bigsby sees *Night and Day* as a companion piece to *Professional Foul;* one examines "the ethical problems generated by a closed society, the other, the moral dilemmas of sustaining a supposedly open society."[7]

Even Mageeba, with his dictatorial control of the Kambawe paper,

formerly owned by a rich Englishman with a title, is allowed to state
his view of the traditional press freedoms of democratic nations. "I
know the British press is very attached to the lobby system. It lets
the journalists and the politicians feel proud of their traditional freedoms while giving the reader as much of the truth as they think is
good for him" (94). Mageeba refers to the colonialist ownership of his
paper as "the voice of an English millionaire" (95). He challenges
Wagner and his fellow journalists to "close ranks and be answerable
to no one but themselves" (96).

In the title of the play, one can find Stoppard's divided arguments.
For Milne, there is as much difference between union and nonunion
philosophies of press freedom and responsibility as there is between
night and day and, ironically for him, between life and death. For
Wagner, there is neither night nor day, but just the cynical grayness
of the seasoned journalist. Similarly, for Carson there is the necessary
juggling of political loyalties in order to guarantee continuation of his
mine. Attempting to bring dictator and rebel together, he sees
Shimbu as wanting the "whole apple" and Mageeba as exploiting his
position by appealing to "the free world about Russian interference."
And when British and Americans protest, Carson asserts, "the Russians will be interfering the stuffing out of Mageeba's army, until
Kambawe is about as independent as Lithuania, and *that* the British
and Americans will protest" (82–83).

It is in Ruth, however, that the moral and political conflicts of the
male journalists, capitalists, and politicians converge, and perhaps it
is in her comment on the futility of Milne's death that Stoppard
makes his statement: "I'm not going to let you think he died for free
speech and the guttering candle of democracy—crap! . . . He died
for the women's page, and the crossword, and the racing results, and
the heartbreak beauty queens and somewhere at the end of a long list
I suppose he died for the leading article too, but it's never worth *that*
. . ." (108).

For Ruth there is only inhumanity in the attitudes and actions of
the men around her, cynics and idealists alike, as she proceeds to create her own context from the surrounding chaos. Her naturalistic ac-
counting of her sordid one-night sexual episode with Wagner in a
London hotel is a brilliant contrast with the scene in which she se-
duces Milne in her fantasy, in his presence. She resumes the grubbi-
ness of reality when at the end she ironically refers to becoming a

tart, an allusion to an earlier conversation with Wagner in which she rejects his description of her as one.

The use of asides only for the character of Ruth gives her special importance in a world where male values dominate. She serves as a commentator on those values. She is also a continuation of the female characters in Stoppard's other works, most notably Jane in *Lord Malquist and Mr. Moon,* Constance in *"M" Is for Moon Among Other Things,* Penelope in *Another Moon Called Earth,* and Dotty in *Jumpers.* As public events unfold or whirl chaotically around them and their husbands ignore their needs, they create their contexts. Only in *The Real Thing* (1982) does this female character reach a full and positive dramatization in Annie. For Annie succeeds not only in arranging her own life but in educating her dramatist-husband. She does change things as the females in Stoppard's previous dramas do not, and, certainly, as Ruth in *Night and Day* does not.

Although it is Milne whose idealism draws the sympathy of the audience and Wagner whose cynicism and cowardice draw contempt, it is Ruth's lament the audience comes away with. For Milne's idealism is self-destructive physically as Wagner's cynicism is morally. Ruth as a Senecan ghost-type hovers impotently over the actions in a male world.

One final comment about characters concerns Stoppard's handling of those with whom he seems to sympathize. Of the antagonistic journalists, the conservative Milne comes off more humanely than does the liberal Wagner, just as George Moore in *Jumpers* and, later, Henry in *The Real Thing* are developed more sympathetically than are their liberal opposites. Stoppard may be ambivalent intellectually as he claims, but emotionally his vote is cast for the conservative whom he develops in full human dimensions in contrast with the one-dimensional portrait of the liberal.

Like Ayer who had responded to Stoppard's characterizations of the logical positivists in *Jumpers,* so a union journalist, "Marc," of the *Sunday Times* comments on Stoppard's conservative position on closed shops in journalism. No secret to those who know him, Stoppard's "argument may have gained ferocity during his talks with his friend and Buckinghamshire neighbour, Paul Johnson, as the play was gestating. Johnson, former *New Statesman* editor, is the man who saw through Socialism to become, in Michael Foot's words, 'Mrs. Thatcher's swooning disciple.' The play is dedicated to him."[8]

If Stoppard does not take positions directly on issues, as he claims, he does so indirectly in the manner in which he unsympathetically develops his liberal characters. The seasoned union journalist Wagner earns our moral repugnance, whereas the young, idealistic Milne, earnestly defending personal and professional freedoms, although shallowly, wins our admiration. If Stoppard does engage both sides of an issue intellectually, emotionally he argues his side by means of character delineation. Wagner joins Archie Jumpers and Brodie, much later, as antagonists not only to their fictional protagonists, but to Stoppard himself. Archie is amoral; Wagner is immoral; Brodie is an aesthetic boor. So although Stoppard's political commitments do not emerge in this or earlier plays, the broad outlines of his sympathies are drawn in *Jumpers* and, even more indirectly, perhaps, in other early works.

Chapter Ten
Minor Stage Plays

Describing *The Real Inspector Hound* and *After Magritte* as an "attempt to bring off a sort of comic coup in pure mechanistic terms,"[1] Stoppard was in effect explaining, at least in part, all of his plays, for the clever setting up of complications—divergences, to use his own term—and then working them into a carefully constructed resolution is for him a problem-solving process. In a number of interviews, he has used the term "nuts and bolts"[2] to characterize the mechanical aspects of plot construction. In these nuts-and-bolts plays, language, visual spectacles, and farce are wedded, resulting in such plays as *After Magritte* and *The Real Inspector Hound.* When ideas prevail over plot, the high comedy of ideas results, as in his three major plays of flashy mind projections: *Rosencrantz and Guildenstern Are Dead, Jumpers,* and *Travesties.* In these literary and highly literate dramas of ideas, the nuts and bolts become metaphoric girders for his intellectual debates. In other plays, such as *Dogg's Hamlet, Cahoot's Macbeth,* plot mechanisms and ideas vie equally with each other for audience attention, sometimes distractingly.

The Real Inspector Hound (1968)

In this, his second publicly performed stage play, plot mechanisms are put in place in a parody of the formulaic *Mousetrap* by Agatha Christie.

The main characters are Higgs, Moon, and Puckeridge (after *Punch's* Muggeridge?), who are first-, second-, and third-string critics. On this night at the theater, Moon, substituting for Higgs, is obsessed with Puckeridge's aspirations to replace him (Moon). A companion-critic for the evening is Birdboot, whose obsession is women, in this case two of the actresses playing that night. Both critics act and talk out their obsessions as they watch the performance of the Christie-like play, complete with the isolated Muldoon Manor, the discovered body, and the appearance of an inspector. Inspector

Hound turns out to be Lady Muldoon's allegedly deceased husband
disguised as the wheelchair-ridden brother of the said husband. In
addition he turns out also to be the critic Puckeridge and, of course,
the detective.

In a manner superficially reminiscent of Pirandello's *Six Characters
in Search of an Author,* in which real life and stage action intermingle,
Birdboot's obsession with actresses Felicity and Cynthia gets the better of him. He jumps on stage to become involved with the drama he
is watching. With the help of Mrs. Drudge, the formulaic maid who
tries to help solve the murders by remembering emotional outbursts
of various suspects who had threatened to murder, each for his own
reasons, Stoppard brings his play to a conclusion. The bodies of
Higgs, Birdboot, and Moon lie on the stage, and Lady Muldoon's
husband of various disguises has both committed and solved the murders. As Inspector Hound and as critic Puckeridge, Lord Muldoon
had lived a double life ever since his loss of memory ten years ago.
Lady Muldoon, whose love for her husband kept her potential suitors
at bay (like the mythological Penelope), is happily reunited with
him. The critics lie dead, shot by Muldoon.

Both Birdboot and Moon, defeated in their obsessions, are stock
Stoppardian characters. Like Mr. Moon in *Lord Malquist and Mr.
Moon,* they are characters to whom things are done, and they can find
no way of withdrawing in style from the chaos around them and in
them. And even though Stoppard parodies second- and third-string
theater critics by investing Moon and Birdboot with personal concerns, in one case the neurotic fear of a professional rival and in the
other sexual fantasies about actresses, there is no reason to believe
that Puckeridge is any better. The difference between the survivor
and the slain is that as a Boot character, Puckeridge acts, while
Higgs, Birdboot, and Moon, as Moon characters, are acted upon.

Stoppard has commented frequently about the Boot character in his
writings. The name derives from the character of William Boot in
Evelyn Waugh's novel *Scoop,* and Stoppard himself used the name as
a pseudonym in his early journalistic years. Frequently allied with a
Moon character who on occasion complements him, Boot is the more
aggressive, whereas the passive Moon is agonized by inner conflicts.
As in those many references to Eliot's Prufrock in *Lord Malquist and
Mr. Moon,* the passive character here does not survive, or, at least, he
is victimized in some way. Later on in *Travesties* Stoppard has Lenin
dividing the world into "Who" and "Whom," those who do and

those to whom it is done. Sometimes the distinctions are not clear and the two are fused into one, their difference consisting only in the degree of aggressiveness in one over the other. "I'm a Moon, myself. . . . Confusingly, I used the name Boot, from Evelyn Waugh, as a pseudonym in journalism, but that was because Waugh's Boot is really a Moon, too."[3]

If his Boot character derives from Waugh, the Moon character goes back to Stoppard's early days in Bristol when he saw Paul Newman in *Left-Handed Gun*.

At one point of this film there's a reflection of the moon in a horse-trough. They're all drunk as far as I remember, and suddenly they shoot the reflection of the moon, the water explodes, and Newman is also shouting the word Moon, which is the name of one of the characters in the film. About this time I was writing the first draft of *The Real Inspector Hound*, and I needed a name for one of these critics. . . . And for one reason or another, Moon is a very good name for the sort of person I write about quite a lot—obviously, he could be called Blenkinsop for you.[4]

The Moons and Boots proliferate in Stoppard's writing, going back as early as George Riley in *Enter A Free Man*. The varied qualities of fantasy, lunacy and, one might add, the mythology of Diana in pure and perverse ways, characterize the Moons and Boots, sometimes as one double character, sometimes as two separate characters. Moon mythology occurs in the many popular songs occurring in the plays, most importantly in *Jumpers*, in which the lunar landings of astronauts have demythologized the moon, and in *Night and Day*, where disillusionment pervades love, politics, and journalism. Stoppard "felt that the destruction of moon mythology . . . would be a sort of minute lobotomy performed on the human race. . . ."[5]

Both as a nuts-and-bolts process of plot construction and as a witty use of Moon and Boot characters, *The Real Inspector Hound* is a precursor of *Jumpers* in which a murder goes unpunished, double identities exist, the formulaic inspector is present, and, above all, moon imagery is strong.

After Magritte (1970)

Produced in tandem with *The Real Inspector Hound* in New York in 1972, *After Magritte* had its London opening (1970) two years after

Stoppard's parody of theater critics and Christie whodunits. The title derives from a visit to a Magritte exhibition at the Tate Gallery by three of the main characters: a husband-wife dance couple and the husband's mother.

But the title more importantly intends a *double entendre*, for the play re-creates the overall style of a famous painting at the Magritte exhibition of 1969: *The Menaced Assassin.* In the work a murdered naked woman lies on a couch. A man's dark coat and hat on a chair, a suitcase alongside, and a man dressed in a black suit looking into the horn of an old-fashioned victrola on a table constitute the remaining images of the room. At the far center of the room there is a window, through which can be seen the heads of three men looking into the room. In the distance beyond them, the peaks of several mountains are visible. But the largest and closest figures in the painting are two men in homburgs—one with a club and the other with a net. They are policemen or detectives, standing, one on each side of the doorway.

In the opening scene of *After Magritte,* a policeman is looking through a window into a disordered room in which the furniture is piled against the door. The mother is lying on an ironing board, covered with a white bath towel with a black bowler hat reposing on her stomach. The daughter-in-law, Thelma Harris, in full-length ball gown, her hair "expensively up," is crawling on the floor. Her husband, dressed in thigh-length green rubber fishing waders and black evening dress trousers is blowing into the recess of a lamp shade. Unlike Magritte's painting, all of Stoppard's tableau has a logical explanation, and it is the purpose of the play to provide it.

But even as this scene is explained, another set of mystifying scenes is posed. For on their way home from the Tate, the three members of the family have witnessed a spectacle, for which each has an explanation totally different from that of the other two. The divergences (Stoppard's term for complications) between the Magritte-like scene and the witnessed spectacle (with its three distinct versions) converge in the course of the play in the final solving of the mystery by the attendant constable. In essence, the problem-solving process of the nuts-and-bolts theory is here at its most mechanically pure, perhaps, of all the stage plays of Stoppard. The play is one long entertaining joke.

The conflict in the play develops from the arguments about whose description of the spectacle is the accurate one. Thelma insists that she saw a one-legged footballer carrying a football. Harris, however, maintains that it was a blind man carrying a white stick with a tortoise. The mother describes him as a hopscotch player in the "loose-fitting striped gaberdine of a convicted felon,"[6] with a handbag under one arm and a cricket bat in the other. Complications begin when Inspector Foot of the Yard (a typical Stoppardian pun) and Constable Holmes appear on the scene, having been notified of a robbery. Their reconstruction of a crime that never happened is explained at the end.

As it turns out, Foot was the one-legged man whom the family saw on their drive home from the Magritte exhibition. In the midst of shaving on that day, he had noted a parking vacancy and hurried out to move his illegally parked car before the warden came around. As he ran out, he grabbed his wife's pocketbook for the meter change and her parasol to keep off the rain.

The explanation for the opening tableau, one finds out in the course of the investigation by Foot and Holmes, is that the couple are getting ready for their evening performance. Thelma is repairing her torn gown and, also, mentions massaging her mother-in-law on the ironing board. Meantime, Harris runs into difficulty as bulbs burn out and he must maneuver counterweights in order to be able to reach the lamp. The absurd spectacle observed by the officer through the window and by the audience observing the goings on is clarified at the end by the inspector.

The two witnessed spectacles of the play have as their basis another scene outside the play that Stoppard provides from his own experience. It concerns a "man he knew who bought a peacock on impulse and, shortly afterward, while shaving in his pajamas, observed the bird escaping from his country garden. Dropping his razor, he set off in pursuit and managed to catch the feathered fugitive just as it reached a main road adjoining his property. At that moment, a car flashed by, middle-aged husband at the wheel, wife at his side. . . . There was, as we know, a perfectly rational explanation."[7]

Details from these scenes are used by Stoppard again in *Jumpers,* in which Inspector Bones, arriving at George Moore's home after receiving a call about a murder, is greeted by George, face covered with shaving cream, tortoise in one hand, and bow and arrow in the other. In this play, also, a rational explanation is provided, but both spectacle and explanation in *Jumpers* are only a part of a complex and very elaborate high comedy of ideas.

Spectacles like those in *After Magritte* are integral to Stoppard's writing, including his only novel. They are a means to an end in his comedies of ideas and as an end in themselves in the nuts-and-bolts farces, for they provide a means of solving problems of plot construction. The plot in *After Magritte* is unencumbered with Moons and Boots or with ideas and intellectual joking. But it is still one grand Stoppardian joke. To attach, as one critic has done, significance to the plot as refutation of the dadaist view of things is perhaps a straining for substance the play does not support.

Dirty Linen and *New-Found-Land* (1976)

Less mechanistic than *The Real Inspector Hound* and *After Magritte* but still joking, this time at the expense of civil servants and the American bicentennial year, *Dirty Linen* contains some of the poetry, fantasy, and linguistic exuberance of Stoppard's major dramas.

On 5 April 1976, American Ed Berman, to whom *Dirty Linen* is dedicated, became a naturalized English citizen. On that same date Stoppard's play opened as an Ambiance Lunch-Hour Theatre Club presentation at Inter-Action's Almost Free Theatre, one of several organizations in which Berman had been very active. Indeed, the description of the American seeking British citizenship in the play-within-a-play, *New-Found-Land,* is that of Berman, whose association with various community arts and action projects, such as the Ambiance Lunch-Hour Theatre Club, the Almost Free Theatre, the Fun Art Bus and the Dogg's Troupe, City Farms 1 in Kentish Town, and youth employment programs, is mentioned at the end of the published play.

"*Dirty Linen* was supposed to be a play to celebrate Ed Berman's naturalization, but it went off in a different direction—*New-Found-Land* was then written to re-introduce the American Connection," writes Stoppard at the beginning of the playbill note.[8] In 1976 America celebrated its bicentennial, and a recording of "The Star Spangled Banner" was a part of the production.

Utilizing a favorite Stoppardian technique, the play within a play, *New-Found-Land* is loosely and unabashedly contained within *Dirty Linen*. The drama is divided into three distinct parts: "Dirty Linen," "New-Found-Land," and "Dirty Linen, Concluded." The link between the inner and outer plays is the technicality of having two committees meet in the same room. One is a select committee to investigate and report on the sex scandals in Parliament that are being exploited in the newspapers, and the other is a two-member committee (of the home secretary's office) meeting to consider the granting of citizenship to an American. At a climactic point in *Dirty Linen* when the sexy secretary has just finished a fantasy speech about various sexual involvements, someone is heard approaching the room and the committee vanishes hurriedly.

Two men, Bernard and Arthur, enter the room for the purpose of conducting their business on the naturalization application. Their meeting, as Stoppard's playwriting technique is wont to do, takes a different direction, and both men fantasize, one about an old five-pound note he had won from Lloyd George and the other about a trip through America, from New York to New England, Chicago, Atlanta, New Orleans, and finally California. As he quotes from a sonnet by Keats "with wondering eyes we stare at the Pacific, and all of us look at each other with a wild surmise—silent,"[9] Arthur is interrupted by the entrance of the first committee, which has arrived to conclude its investigation. Protesting their expulsion from the room, the two home office men are overruled by their home secretary, who has now joined the select committee investigating the sexual scandal.

The play ends with the committee's cover-up of the scandal without any investigation at all. Instead, they blame the press for exploiting the sensational disclosures. The committee concludes that "it is the just and proper expectation of every Member of Parliament, no less than for every citizen of this country, that what they choose to do in their own time, and with whom, is . . . between them and their conscience . . . provided they do not transgress the rights of others or the law of the land; and that this principle is not to be sacrificed to that Fleet Street Stalking-horse masquerading as a sacred cow labelled 'The People's Right to Know' "(72).

Dramatizing political scandals that were fresh in the minds of audiences in both England and America, Stoppard writes a satire about the defensive tactics of the select committee and also two entertaining fantasy monologues. The British fascination with political sex scandals and America's with money and power scandals had just been illustrated in the Profumo case and the Nixon-Watergate upheaval respectively.

In the two plays, Stoppard has brought off successfully his problem-solving technique in the intertwining of two very different subjects: Berman's naturalization and the bureaucratic workings of an investigative committee. The connection between the two stories is more mechanical than that in *The Real Inspector Hound*, in which the paranoiac Moon walks on the stage to answer the telephone and thus involves himself and Birdboot in the proceedings of the play within a play, carrying that drama into the plane of the surreal. In *Dirty Linen* and *New-Found-Land*, the plot action remains realistic throughout.

But the realism is deceptive as one sees images and hears rhythms more commonly associated with the language of Ionesco and Pinter. The sex scandals focus on a fashionable eating place, the *Coq d'Or*. One of the M.P.'s on the committee is Cocklebury-Smythe. At one point, he tells Maddie, the secretary, that if she were asked where she had "lunch on Friday, breakfast on Saturday or dinner on Sunday, best thing is to forget Crockford's, Claridge's and the *Coq d'Or*" (23). In an attempt to forget the names, Maddie keeps repeating them, making mistakes and being corrected until there results a dazzling display of sounds in the sexual double entendres that take over. As the members of the committee confess their favorite hangouts, the style evokes Ionesco's *The Bald Soprano* in which Mr. and Mrs. Smith by the process of logical deduction discover that they are man and wife. Here are just some of the passages in *Dirty Linen*:

> CHAMBERLAIN: I was at the Crock of Gold, Selfridges and the Green Cockatoo.
>
> . . .
>
> WITTENSHAW: I was at the Cross Cook, the Fighting Cocks, the Green Door, the Crooked Grin and the Golden Carriages.
>
> . . .
>
> COCKLEBURY-SMYTHE: I forgot—I was at the Golden Carriages as well as Claridges, and the Odd Sock and the Cocked Hat.
>
> WITTENSHAW: I didn't see you at the Cocked Hat—I went on to the Cox and Box. (49)

Maddie turns out to be the mystery woman, of course, and the obfuscations of the accusations eventually lead to the general disclaimer in the statement at the end of the play.

Similar fantasy exists in the monologues by Bernard and Arthur in *New-Found-Land*, particularly the latter, as he is asked whether he knows America at all. He responds with "My America!—my new-found-land!" He then traces a journey beginning with the Statue of Liberty's appeal to the huddled masses, moving on to Manhattan

"ablaze like jewels as a million windows give back the setting sun,"
then a ride on the Silver Chief through Chicago, where "tight-lipped
men in tight-buttoned overcoats and grey fedoras join the poker
games," to Kentucky, where "blue skies and grass are as one on the
azure horizon," to Atlanta, which is still burning, to New Orleans's
French quarter, where "the sun hangs like a copper pan over boarding
houses with elaborately scrolled gingerbread eaves," on the Galveston
train, where "the whole car—Bible salesmen, buck privates from Fort
Dixie, majorettes from L.S.U., farm boys and a couple of nuns—is
singing the blues in the night" (60–65).

The fantasy ends on the California coast, a veritable paradise of
"vineyards and orchards, a sun-bathed Canaan decked with peach and
apricot, apples, plums, citrus fruit and pomegranates, which grow to
the very walls of pink and yellow bungalows to the very edge of
swimming pools where near-naked goddesses with honey-brown skins
rub oil into their long downy limbs" (65).

The monologue-journey concludes with a question: "Could this be
paradise or is it, after all, purgatory?" (65). The question is answered
in the surrealistically purgatorial scene in which

picture palaces rise from the plain, search lights and letters of fire light up
the sky, and a screaming hydra-headed mob surges, fighting and weeping,
around an unseen idol—golden calf or Cadillac, we do not stop to see—for
now beyond the city, beyond America, beyond all, nothing lies before us
but an endless expanse of blue, flecked with cheerful whitecaps. With wondering eyes we stare at the Pacific, and all of us look at each other with wild
surmise—silent. (65)

With this last line, a borrowing from Keats's sonnet "On First
Looking into Chapman's Homer," the select committee on sex scandals barges into the room to claim it for their meeting. Then follows
a report in which the committee, using bureaucratic jargon, concludes that "no evidence or even suggestion of laws broken or harm
done" (72) has been found.

Stylistically the fantasies, sexual and utopian, wipe out the realistic
framework of the drama. For those interested in the plot, the entertainment is there; for those caught up in the language fantasies of the
M.P.'s and of Arthur, the reward consists of the images conjured and
the rhythms of the language. Indeed, in a parody of himself, Stoppard has Bernard sleeping through most of Arthur's imaginary journey through America, waking up at the Texas points of Arthur's trip.

Chapter Eleven
Political Plays

Stoppard's four clearly political plays—*Every Good Boy Deserves Favour, Professional Foul* (television), *Dogg's Hamlet, Cahoot's Macbeth,* and *Squaring the Circle* (television)—were as inevitable as his writing about journalists.

They are not, however, without their precursors, *The Gamblers,* a stage drama produced at the University of Bristol in 1965, and *Neutral Ground,* a television drama produced by Granada Television in 1968, deal with political prisoners and Eastern European spies respectively.

Not until the late 1970s, however, in a review of Paul Johnson's *Enemies of Society,* does Stoppard express his political position in support of a "Western liberal democracy favouring an intellectual elite and a progressive middle class . . . based on a moral order derived from Christian absolutes."[1] He clearly distinguishes between the kind of totalitarian regime in pre-1917 Russia and that in power since the revolution. "The great irony about Marx was that his impulses were deeply moral while his intellect insisted on a materialistic view of the world. . . . Lenin perverted Marxism, and Stalin carried on from there."[2]

The matter of human freedom—personal, as in the case of George Riley in *Enter a Free Man,* or political, as in the plays discussed in this chapter—is deeply ingrained in Stoppard's characters. Stoppard notes in his interview with *Theatre Quarterly* editors that while Lenin "was in a Tsarist prison, and in Tsarist exile, he managed to research and write his book on the development of capitalism in Russia, and receive books and magazines, and write to friends, all that, whereas—well, compare Solzhenitsyn."[3] Human solidarity is preferable to class solidarity, and arguments between hard and soft radicals today are not about tactics, as they claim, but about philosophy, so Stoppard maintains.

The inevitability of political dramas by Stoppard is due, along with his Eastern European human rights activism, at least in part, to his pique at the constant criticism that his plays were not serious and that he lacked social commitment. "So I'd like to write a play—say, XYZ—which would pertain to anything from a Latin American coup to the British left, and probably when I've done it I'll still be asked why I don't write political plays."[4]

Two of the four political plays, *Professional Foul* and *Squaring the Circle*, are discussed here because of their subject matter, even though they were written for television. Their realistic and documentary styles contrast sharply with the surrealism of the other two, partly because they are intended for a different medium.

All four dramas deal directly with the issue of free speech in Eastern bloc countries. *Professional Foul* argues the subject intellectually; *Every Good Boy Deserves Favour* demonstrates the consequences of political dissidence; *Dogg's Hamlet, Cahoot's Macbeth* dramatizes a situational dissidence that may well lead to those consequences; and *Squaring the Circle* in documentary style depicts the impasse at which both the oppressed and the oppressor have arrived. In *Every Good Boy Deserves Favour* and *Dogg's Hamlet, Cahoot's Macbeth*, language is not only used for its own brilliance, but as the very subject of that brilliance. As such, language is a weapon for power. The Le Carré-like spy intrigue of *Professional Foul* ends happily for all, but the action of the intrigue diminishes the argument of the play, and, thereby, its language. However, the brilliantly devised abuse of language in *Every Good Boy Deserves Favour* and *Dogg's Hamlet, Cahoot's Macbeth* and the counterattack on that abuse by a prisoner and his son in one drama and by a group of actors in the other give language new dimensions as a weapon of political power.

Every Good Boy Deserves Favour (1977)

Of Stoppard's short stage plays, *Every Good Boy Deserves Favour* occupies a unique position for a number of reasons. First, its auspicious premiere at the Royal Festival Hall on 1 July 1977 launched the John Player Centenary Festival. If one wonders why a short play should be produced in a huge concert hall rather than an intimate theater, the explanation is that the eighty-piece London Symphony Orchestra was listed as a character in this "piece for actors and orchestra," the subtitle of the play. With a considerably reduced orchestra and a different cast, the play later enjoyed an extended run at the Mermaid Theatre. Then from 30 July to 4 August 1979, the play was performed at the Metropolitan Opera House in New York with full orchestra.

The play's uniqueness lies also in its being Stoppard's first stage play to deal directly with a commitment of the author to a cause, the cause in this case being human rights. Charged frequently by critics with a lack of commitment to social, moral, or philosophical causes, Stoppard has repeatedly rejected absolute stances. He considers himself a "conservative with a small c,"[5] in politics, literature, education, and theater, but he rejects ideology and dogma. Furthermore, he says that both characters in the pairs of Rosencrantz and Guildenstern, James Joyce and Tristan Tzara, George Moore and Archibald Jumpers speak for him. Temperamentally and intellectually he is very much on Joyce's side, and he embraces the morality of George Moore. "I tend to write for two people rather than for One Voice."[6]

In *Every Good Boy Deserves Favour*, however, one strong, clear voice does emerge for the first time in Stoppard's writing. But it is a voice that never sacrifices entertainment and aesthetic values to didactic style. Indeed, the dialogue crackles with wit as the play takes on the tone of a contemporary fable. Although not quite a play that will find its way "into the Peter and the Wolf repertory,"[7] Irving Wardle of the *Times* considers it a "great waste if it vanishes after a single performance."[8] Bernard Levin of the *Sunday Times* writes that "the play makes us laugh even as we rage," and he draws a comparison with "A Modest Proposal," saying that "Stoppard's sword and wit alike are as keen and deadly as Swift's."[9]

The circumstances surrounding the play contribute to its uniqueness. At the time *Every Good Boy Deserves Favour* came to New York in 1979, London theatergoers had their choice of "four Stoppards." *Night and Day, Undiscovered Country, Dirty Linen,* and *Dogg's Hamlet, Cahoot's Macbeth* were on the boards, and Stoppard had written the screenplay for *The Human Factor*, Graham Greene's novel.

But with all his professional activity, Stoppard was reading books and articles by and about Russian dissidents. He had met a Russian exile, Victor Fainberg, who had been imprisoned for protesting against the invasion of Czechoslovakia in 1968.[10] In one of two long monologues by Alexander Ivanov in *Every Good Boy Deserves Favour*, Stoppard includes a reference to a trial that "took place on August the twenty-first of 1968, and in the courtroom it was learned that the Russian army had gone to the aid of Czechoslovakia."[11]

Stoppard's own explanation of the genesis of the play, after an invitation in 1974 from André Previn to write a piece that could be performed with a full orchestra on stage, is contained in an interview with Mel Gussow in 1979:

I wasn't sitting there saying I want to write about a Russian dissident. I had to write a play for a small number of actors and a large orchestra. At first I decided that it would be about a zillionaire who had his own orchestra; after supper, the musicians would troop in to play. Then I thought, he could be a zillionaire who thinks he has an orchestra.

Once the Orchestra was in his imagination, he didn't have to be a zillinaire, he could be a lunatic. Coincidentally, I read about people locked away in asylums for political reasons. Suddenly the subject matter seemed appropriate to the form: the dissident is a discordant note in a highly orchestrated society.[12]

And so, with André Previn conducting the eighty-piece London Symphony Orchestra, the play premiered at the Royal Festival Hall on 1 July 1977.

The main characters of this fifty-minute play are two Ivanovs (one named Alexander Ivanov, the other called simply Ivanov) committed to an insane asylum in Eastern Europe. The action occurs in three playing areas: a cell, an office, and a school. Scenes change by means of lighting. Alexander is a political prisoner, whereas Ivanov is a mental patient. The latter's insanity takes the form of fantasies about conducting an orchestra. Insisting that he hears music, Ivanov plays a triangle as part of an orchestra. The conditions for the release of the two men are that the lunatic admit that he does not have an orchestra and that the political patient admit that no Soviet doctor would put a sane man into a lunatic asylum.

The releases occur when a colonel appears (replacing the ubiquitous inspectors of Stoppard's other dramas) and, in his confusion about the identities of the two prisoners, addresses each with the question intended for the other. Consequently, Ivanov admits that he shouldn't think that a sane man would be so incarcerated, and Alexander Ivanov denies that he has an orchestra or that he hears music of any kind. Each responds positively when asked how he feels. Instructing the doctor to get the men out of the asylum as there was absolutely nothing wrong with them, the colonel leaves, as do Alexander and his son Sacha, who has come to visit his father. Ivanov, however, takes his triangle and joins the percussion section, and the doctor joins in with his violin. Sacha in the last lines of the play sings: "Papa, don't be crazy! Everything can be all right!" (39).

The plot is simple enough, but its development involves, as Irving Wardle has put it, "the clearest instance so far of Stoppard's capacity to express social indignation and a firm moral viewpoint through the kind of intellectual gymnastics and formal trickery which are often considered the marks of flippant detachment."[13] Central to the Stoppardian trickery is the use of the orchestra and its lunatic triangle player and conductor as a metaphor for a fantasy world.

From time to time the lunatic makes critical judgments about the poor performances of the imagined cellos or the horns, and he invites opinions from Alexander. Alexander keeps insisting that he is no judge of music, that he does not play an instrument, until in frustration Ivanov asks, "What the hell are you doing here?" When told that the reason is slander, Ivanov berates his cell-mate: "What a fool! Never speak ill of a musician—those bastards won't rest. They're animals" (13). He totally ignores Alexander's repeated statements about the political basis for his internment. One short monologue of Ivanov's is a masterpiece of Stoppardian language wizardry and at the same time a richly ironic metaphor for the system that has incarcerated both men:

You can speak frankly. You will find I am without prejudice. I have invited musicians *into my own house*. And do you know why? Because we all have some musician in us. Any man says he has no musician in him, I'll call that man a *bigot*. Listen, I've had clarinet players eating *at my own table*. I've had French whores and gigolos speak to me in the *public street*, I mean horns, I mean piccolos, so don't worry about me, maestro, I've sat down with them, *drummers* even sharing a plate of tagliatelle Verdi and stuffed Puccini—why I know people who make the orchestra eat in the kitchen, off scraps, the way you'd throw a trombone to a dog, I mean a second violinist, I mean to the lions; I love musicians, I respect them, human beings to a man. Let me put it like this: if I smashed this instrument of yours over your head would you need a carpenter, a welder, or a brain surgeon? (12–13)

Although Ivanov plays his triangle at frequent intervals whenever the orchestra plays, his is usually a subversive triangle and the percussion performance goes wrong. The music then stops, and the scene may shift, as it does at one point, to the schoolroom, where Alexander's son Sacha is being taught to play a triangle and where the music lesson then changes into one in geometry. In his responses to the teacher's questions, like his father, Sacha gives apolitical answers. In stichomythic style, the questions eventually involve Sacha's father. After writing that "a triangle is the polygon bounded by the fewest possible sides," Sacha asks: "Is this what they make papa do?"(16).

Scenes between the two prisoners, between Sacha and his teacher, and between Sacha and his father are alternated with those between the doctor and the two prisoners. In a ludicrous twist, Stoppard has the doctor, like his lunatic patient, obsessed with an instrument. His is a violin. Although following the official line of argument in trying to convince Alexander that the sane are outside the asylum and the insane are inside, the doctor is fairly mild in his treatment of his patients. He informs Alexander, at one point, that the "Colonel or rather Doctor Rozinsky" who has now taken over his case is not a psychiatrist but a doctor of philosophy.

Having heard Alexander's long story of his arrest for merely writing to various people about a friend who was in prison, the doctor picks up his violin, and, plucking *E G B D F*, says about Alexander's son Sacha, "He's a good boy. He deserves a father" (28). And another schoolroom scene commences. This time the doctor enters, and Sacha pleads for the release of his father. The play's title derives from this scene.

In the final scene, the colonel, in a mistaken identification of the two prisoners, discovers that both are cured. The conclusion one can draw is that repressive institutions, if they fall, may do so from the weight of their own bureaucratic bungling. In the bungling of the minor officials, the dead language is heavy indeed.

Professional Foul (1977)

In a *Theatre Quarterly* interview, Stoppard speaks of *Jumpers* as going "against Marxist-Leninism in particular, and against all materialistic philosophy. I believe all political acts must be judged in moral terms, in terms of their consequences. Otherwise they are simply attempts to put the boot on some other foot. There is a sense in which contradictory political arguments are restatements of each other. For example, Leninism and Fascism are restatements of totalitarianism." He comments that Leninism "in action after 1917 was very much worse than anything which had gone on in Tsarist Russia."[14]

In speaking of political plays, he classifies three kinds: those "which are about specific situations," those "about a general political situation," and those "which are *political acts* in themselves." Political acts he describes as "attacking or insulting or shocking an audience."[15]

Stoppard's personal involvement in political activity took the form of an address at a rally in Trafalgar Square in 1976, organized by the Committee Against Psychiatric Abuse. The rally was followed by a march to the Soviet embassy to protest mental homes as punishment camps. Then in February 1977, he visited Moscow in conjunction with Amnesty International, and in June of that year he travelled to his native Czechoslovakia for the first time since he and his family left during the Hitler era. He spoke with Czech dramatist Vaclav Havel, whom Kenneth Tynan calls Stoppard's doppelgänger. Recently released from prison, Havel is the person in whose situation Stoppard might have been had his father's firm not moved the family to Singapore.

In September 1977, still another political play by Stoppard was aired on British television: *Professional Foul.* Like Stoppard's realistic dramas—*Enter A Free Man* and, later, *Night and Day* and *The Real Thing*—*Professional Foul* does not have linguistic or visual fireworks.

At the center of the action is a series of games that are being played. One of the games is a soccer match between England and Czechoslovakia, the other the games journalists play to get a story teletyped home. The most important game of all is that played by a J. Stuart Mill Professor of Philosophy at Cambridge and his former Czech student.

Once more Stoppard dramatizes a situation of philosophers arguing matters of ethics. George Moore, Duncan McFee, and Archibald Jumpers of *Jumpers* are reinvented in another trio: Anderson of Cambridge; McKendrick, a self-styled Marxist of Stoke; and Chetwyn, who constantly reverts to Greek tragedy for his view of morality. All three are attending a symposium in Prague. Anderson has also planned to attend the soccer match, having long been a devotee of the sport. The conflict of the drama arises when Anderson, who is the guest of the Czech government, experiences a clash between his responsibility to his host and a larger responsibility to a former Czech student of his who wants Anderson to smuggle to England a paper on human rights. The former student, Hollar, has a son, Sasha (also named Alexander, like the names in *Every Good Boy Deserves Favour*).

In spy thriller fashion, Anderson meets the wife and the son of Hollar, after Hollar has been taken away by the police. Following adventures with the police and with the British journalists, Anderson secretly hides the manuscript in the briefcase of McKendrick, guessing that the latter would be the one least likely to be searched by customs. His plan succeeds, and, as David Pryce-Jones writes, there is "a happy ending, then, almost slapstick, with its immensely satisfying symmetry."[16]

After Anderson has his own experiences with the police and has been prevented from seeing the soccer match as a result, he changes his scheduled address to the gathering of philosophers and, instead, lectures on human rights. Upset by the change, the authorities ring the fire alarm, concluding the conference and the visit of the English academicians. Anderson's former reluctance to violate the hospitality of his host gives way to a larger ethical issue, that of freedom of expression. Hollar suggests that if Anderson didn't know he was smuggling the manuscript, he would not be in violation of his ethical principles. Taught by his former student, Anderson acts on the suggestion when he hides the paper in McKendrick's briefcase without the knowledge of his colleague.

The title *Professional Foul* derives from a soccer term meaning a necessary and deliberate foul that the soccer players commit in the match. Although the English athletes lose their game to Czechoslovakia, Anderson wins his, even though he had to commit a professional moral foul to do so.

In the drama, Stoppard indulges himself in the philosophical arguing that constitutes the subject of his major plays. One object of his satire is an American academic, Stone, who drones on and on about the ambiguity of language, even as larger moral issues of freedom to use language are being played out by Anderson and Hollar. Philosophical jumperism, like that in *Jumpers*, is carried on by both the traditionalist, Anderson, and the Marxist, McKendrick.

The language joking here is not nearly as colorful as in most of Stoppard's plays, but there is some that reminds one of the usual language games. For example, McKendrick comments that Anderson's picture in the symposium brochure is one of a younger man, to which Anderson replies that it must be an old photograph. Commenting on the oddness of words, Anderson continues: "Young therefore old. Old therefore young. Only odd at first glance."[17]

In an argument over the professional foul that Roy Broadbent, a soccer player, had committed that day, McKendrick argues against the whole ethos of game playing and fouls. At one point in the argument he turns on Chamberlain, a reporter, who had recommended a conclusion to the long evening: "I'm surprised at you, Chamberlain—your newspaper is no hypocritical tabloid tut-tutting yob violence on one page and whipping it up on the other—you write for clergymen and army widows, missionaries, dons, anthropologists . . . you should take an interest—have a drink" (107).

The ethics of philosophers, the deliberate fouls of soccer players, and the disinterestedness of journalists are the subjects of the games played by these British visitors to Prague. *Professional Foul* creatively and purposefully combines the academics and athletes of the earlier *Jumpers* with concern about repressive political systems. Criticism of repression, whether personal, domestic, intellectual, or aesthetic, is a cause to which all of Stoppard's plays are addressed. In *Professional Foul* the repression is that of a particular political system.

In regard to the appearance of his name in an advertisement supporting Ronald Reagan's decision to invade Grenada in 1983, Stoppard commented that he did not sign his name, but that it was there because of his belonging to "the Committee for the Free World, a neo-conservative international organization created 'to mount a defense of . . . Western democratic society.' " He said that moral neutrality can't "justify going into somebody else's country. The question is, is the standpoint of moral neutrality the moral position?"[18] Stoppard's defense of Reagan's position is the same as that used by the philosopher in *Professional Foul*. The game metaphor of the necessity of committing a deliberate foul seems to be his position.

Dogg's Hamlet, Cahoot's Macbeth (1979)

Dogg's Hamlet, Cahoot's Macbeth is the longest of those Stoppardian plays included among his nonmajor works. If, as Tynan asserts, *Lord Malquist and Mr. Moon* is the author's purest expression of his philosophy, one may claim *Dogg's Hamlet, Cahoot's Macbeth* as an example of his quintessential plotting style.

Like *Rosencrantz and Guildenstern Are Dead* whose origins can be traced to an earlier playlet (*Rosencrantz and Guildenstern Meet King Lear*, conceived during Stoppard's early years in Germany on a Ford grant), *Dogg's Hamlet, Cahoot's Macbeth* has origins in two earlier short plays, *Dogg's Our Pet* (1971) and *The (15 Minute) Dogg's Troupe Hamlet* (1975). *Dogg's Our Pet* is an anagram for Dogg's Troupe, Ed Berman's Inter-Action players who performed both of these short plays, the first at the Almost Free Theatre and the second on the terraces of the National Theatre on the South Bank. Berman is the American whose English naturalization is honored in *New-Found-Land*. Berman himself is Professor Dogg, a character in the play.

Dedicated to Dogg and his troupe and to Pavel Kohout, the Czech dramatist, *Dogg's Hamlet, Cahoot's Macbeth* was presented by the British American Repertory Company (BARC) at Warwick University, directed by Berman, in 1979. Berman has long been connected with Inter-Action Productions, a cluster of theatrical groups involved with a number of Stoppard's plays: *After Magritte, Dogg's Our Pet, The (15 Minute) Dogg's Troupe Hamlet, Dirty Linen,* and *New-Found-Land,* and, of course, *Dogg's Hamlet, Cahoot's Macbeth.*

In *Dogg's Hamlet, Cahoot's Macbeth*, Stoppard returns to *Hamlet*, the scene of his first smash hit, *Rosencrantz and Guildenstern Are Dead*, even though his two by-now famous heroes do not appear in this more recent version. He compounds his return to Shakespeare with a playlet in act 2 from *Macbeth*. Both the *Hamlet* and *Macbeth* components of Stoppard's latest adaptation of Shakespeare are very brief and intense condensations of the main actions of the originals.

In a dramatic sleight of hand, Stoppard in act 1 employs the *Hamlet* portion as the play within a play. In act 2, however, he uses the *Macbeth* truncation as the outer play, within which another drama, that of the plight of Czechoslovakian actors and actresses, is contained. In both acts, the actors play double roles: as characters playing a role and as themselves in real life. In act 1 schoolboys erect an acting platform, and in act 2 Landovsky, Chramostova, and Cahoot (a spelling variant of Pavel Kohout's name) perform a shortened *Macbeth* in the living room of a home. Each of the two groups is involved in a truncated production of Shakespeare, in one case *Hamlet* and in the other *Macbeth*. The resulting symmetry of the plot is a subtle coherence of two plays that at first seem to be unrelated. Indeed, Felicia Londré in her study of Stoppard's plays considers *Dogg's Hamlet* separately from *Cahoot's Macbeth*. There is, however, a close connection between the two.

The usual Stoppardian daring to combine two different plays in one is purposeful, for the opening *Hamlet* is a necessary progression to the concluding *Macbeth* segment. Although act 2 seems to begin with an abrupt and complete change of subject matter in its surrealistic shift to a living room in which *Macbeth* is being performed (as was actually done by Pavel Kohout in Czechoslovakia), the shift is deceptive, for the effects of tyranny in Claudius in act 1 and Macbeth in act 2 parallel those of the nameless inspector of contemporary Prague.

The literal connection between the two acts is Easy, a lorry (truck) driver who serves as a link by his appearance in both acts. In the first he is confused by the Dogg language of the schoolboys, but by the end of the second act, he has fallen into the doggerel. Thus, he is able to provide the Czech actors with the Dogg handbook and act as Stoppard's means of having the living room *Macbeth* get round the political censor. Stoppard's structural coup is masterfully executed.

In the confusing melange of role playing—schoolboys as themselves and as Shakespearean actors, Czech actors as themselves and as actors, and Easy (Professor Dogg) as Shakespeare himself—one experiences the totally freewheeling, yet carefully designed, lunacy of Stoppard at his purest. The farce, however, is deadly serious. The usual dislocated characters, their Magritte-like situations and Wittgensteinian language games, and the witty intellectual debates combine with the repressive abuse of language as a political weapon. The problem-solving, entertaining nuts-and-bolts of plot construction are put to a use that turns the gay, schoolboy atmosphere to a somber grey. The drama has the same strangely ambivalent ending as does *Every Good Boy Deserves Favour*.

Act 1 (entitled *Dogg's Hamlet*) begins with a scene reminiscent of the opening scenes of *Rosencrantz and Guildenstern Are Dead*. Instead of what seems to be an interminable spinning of coins in the earlier play, however, there is now a group of schoolboys engaged in playing ball and giving signals to each other by means of their code language. "Brick" means "here"; "cube" means "thanks"; "block" means "next"; "breakfast, breakfast" means "testing, testing"; "sun, dock, trog, slack, pan, sock, slight, bright, none, tun, what, dunce" means "one, two, three, four, five, six, seven, eight, nine, ten, eleven, twelve," and "artichoke" means "lorry." Lines such as "Begat perambulate this aerodrome chocolate eclair found"[19] fill the text until Easy, the lorry driver, appears on the scene with his red carpet and box of small flags and enlists the aid of the schoolboys in constructing the platform to be used for the prize-giving ceremony and the *Hamlet* performance.

The ball-playing code language is now transferred to the work at hand, and the boys form a human chain to pass planks, blocks, and slabs. Easy is discomfited when, upon calling for a plank, he is given a block. He passes it back, and eventually these are used to form the wall. Some blocks have letters printed on them, and when the wall is finished it reads:

> MATHS
> OLD
> EGG (20)

In a scuffle between Easy and Dogg, the wall disintegrates as Easy is knocked through it. When rearranged it reads:

> MEG
> SHOT
> GLAD (21)

The prizes are then handed out by a character named Lady; the recipient of all the prizes is a character named Fox. Easy once more finds himself going through the wall, and his resentment of Dogg is shared by the schoolboys, and all hurl insults at the headmaster as he leaves the stage. When the wall is rearranged once more, it reads

> DOGGS
> HAM
> LET (27)

Dogg reappears as Shakespeare in a realignment of various lines from *Hamlet* to pronounce the prologue:

> For this relief, much thanks.
> Though I am native here, and to the manner born,
> It is a custom more honoured in the breach
> than in the observance
> Well.
> Something is rotten in the state of Denmark.
> To be, or not to be, that is the question.
> There are more things in heaven and earth
> Than are dreamt of in your philosophy—
> There's a divinity that shapes our ends,

Rough hew them how we will
Though this be madness, yet there is method in it.
I must be cruel only to be kind;
Hold, as t'were, the mirror up to nature,
A countenance more in sorrow than in anger.

(28)

Following the prologue, *The (15 Minute) Dogg's Troupe Hamlet* is performed in Shakespearean language, only in two parts, the first consisting of a ten-page truncation in which Hamlet dies and Fortinbras comes on, as in Shakespeare. Then in a further two-page truncation an encore is presented. During the curtain call, Easy walks on stage to retrieve a cube, turning to the audience on the last word, "Cube."

Dogg language, Shakespearean language, and modern English as spoken by Easy when he first appears on stage exist side by side in an ingeniously contrived game of language played by schoolboys. There is audience fascination in the assembling of something on stage, much like the assembly and disassembly of the wedding tent in David Storey's *The Contractor*, as Londré has pointed out in her book on Stoppard.[20] It is the same fascination with which one watches McCann in Pinter's *The Birthday Party* as he carefully tears newspaper column after newspaper column from the top of the page to the bottom. Stoppard's human chain of schoolboys as they pass planks, cubes, and blocks along in the construction of the steps and the wall creates a similar effect.

The integration of Dogg language with this activity gradually accustoms the audience to the inflections in their speech and, consequently, to the meanings realized by the inflections. The language games and jokes harmlessly indulged in by schoolboys in act 1 are a necessary prelude to the more serious games played in act 2 by the Czechoslovakian performers.

In a dislocating realignment in act 2, the audience is abruptly taken from the schoolboy *Hamlet* playlet into a performance of *Macbeth* by Czech actors and actresses in the living room of a house. Stoppard's ambush for the audience is deadly serious. In this act, the *Macbeth* playlet serves as the framework for an inner play. When the actors reach the porter-knocking scene of *Macbeth*, the inner play is introduced with the appearance of an inspector rather than the Shakespearean porter. And unlike Inspector Bones of *Jumpers* or Inspector

Hound of *The Real Inspector Hound* or Inspector Foot of the Yard in *After Magritte*, the inspector here is nameless. The crime he comes to investigate is not murder but one against the state, perpetrated by an acting company that dares to perform *Macbeth* in the living room of a home. Actors step out of their roles and speak as in a debate on the issue of free speech. When they do, we discover that they are Landovsky, Chramostova, and Cahoot.

In the front matter of the published play, Stoppard talks about these performers and about his acquaintance with Pavel Kohout. Having met Kohout and Landovsky on his visit to Czechoslovakia in 1977, Stoppard heard from the playwright a year later about a Living-Room Theatre (LRT): "Pavel Landovsky and Vlasta Chramostova are starring Macbeth and Lady, a well known and forbidden young singer Vlastimil Tresnak is singing Malcolm and making music, one young girl who couldn't study the theatre-school, Tereza Kohoutova, by chance my daughter, is playing little parts and reading remarks; and the last man, that's me . . .! is reading a little bit playing the rest of the roles, on behalf of his great colleague" (3).

Although "inspired by these events," Stoppard says, "Cahoot is not Kohout, and this necessarily over-truncated *Macbeth* is not supposed to be a fair representation of Kohout's elegant seventy-five minute version" (3). Yet the play on names is obvious.

The room in which *Macbeth* is being performed is bugged, and at intervals the inspector receives a call from a colleague who inquires about the situation. He responds, "How the hell do I know? But if it's not free expression, I don't know what is!" (73).

The interruption of the performance by the inspector and the ensuing debate on free speech reach a climax when Easy reappears just after Macduff's flight to England has been announced. Easy hands the hostess his phrase book of code Dogg language, and the performance continues, with Shakespearean language alternated with Dogg, leaving the inspector befuddled and excited as he exclaims to his telephone caller that the group should have ten years minimum for acting out of hostility to the republic. As Dogg, in the role of Shakespeare, speaks the prologue in the *Hamlet* play, so the inspector addresses the group with: "Thank you! Thank you! Thank you! Thank you! Scabs! Stinking slobs—crooks. You're nicked, Jock. Punks make me puke. Kick back, I'll break necks, smack chops, put yobs in padlocks and fix facts. Clamp down on poncy gits like a ton of bricks" (76). Without realizing it he has picked up some Dogg, thus illustrating the hostess's earlier comment that one doesn't learn Dogg, but only catches it. He then shouts to Boris and Doris (Landovsky and Chramostova) to hand him gray slabs, and as in act 1 the platform is built. The idea of a repressive wall takes over here as the performers conclude with Malcolm's lines:

> Alabaster ominous nifty, blanket noon
> Howl cinder trellis pistols owl by scone.
> (So, thanks to all at once and to each one,
> Whom we invite to see us crowned at Scone.)
> (77)

Over the fanfare Easy comments: "Double double. Double double toil and trouble. No. Shakespeare. (*Silence*) Well, it's been a funny sort of week. But I should be back by Tuesday" (77).

Stoppard's love of language games is consummately realized in this play, as nonsense doggerel, Shakespearean eloquence, and abused language of repressive political systems combine to create a Pirandellian world of illusion and reality. Just as the political prisoner and his son Sasha, having stood their ground in *Every Good Boy Deserves Favour*, are freed, only because of bureaucratic bumbling, into the world that imprisoned them in the first place, so Easy and the Czech actors resume their real-life roles at the conclusion of *Cahoot's Macbeth*. The normal worlds to which all return are not those, as in Shakespearean dramas, purified of evil or resumed after disruption. They are worlds in which the human spirit survives the immediate problem without in any way solving it, except to keep that spirit intact.

In a larger sense, one may see Easy as the Moon character in act 1, the person who is acted on, transformed in act 2 into a Boot character, the person who acts. The inspector, on the other hand, is a Boot (with a little Moon in him as he is confused by what he doesn't understand), and the Czech actors are Moons who, with the help of Easy, take on positive Boot qualities and, thereby, are able to carry on.

Shakespeare's *Hamlet* and *Macbeth* dramatize the corruption of power by tyrants and the eventual restitution of society to the forces of good. Stoppard's drama, however, deals with the abuse of language as a means of continuing power and views social restitution as consisting only in the ability of the individual to resist tyranny for himself.

Squaring the Circle (1984)

Suggested by film producer Fred Broggers in 1982 and later described by Stoppard as a "personal dramatized essay," *Squaring the Circle*, a television play about the history of the Solidarity union in Poland, attempts to show the irreconcilability of Solidarity's definition of freedom with that of the communist bloc of Eastern European nations. The two definitions are not only irreconcilable, Stoppard asserts, but incapable of coexisting. In the absolute sense of the logician or mathematician, a circle cannot be turned into a square with the same area.

Stoppard divides his essay into four parts (not acts) entitled "The First Secretary," "Solidarity," "Congress," and "The General." To the real life characters of Leonid Brezhnev, Edward Gierek, Wojciech Jaruzelski, Lech Walesa, and others, he adds a fictional American narrator and a witness. Like Carr in *Travesties*, the narrator serves as a filtering consciousness for the events. The ponderous language of the communist officials recalls that of Lenin, also in *Travesties*, but only as bureaucratic mimicry. Expectedly there are the tricks of the stage and linguistics employed in Stoppard's other dramas. These reach a climax near the end in an invented card game played by the communist Jaruzelski, the bishop Glemp, and the unionist Walesa. Like the acrobats of *Jumpers* and the fictional architect's house of cards contained within the fictional play *House of Cards* in *The Real Thing*, the card game is a metaphor for the entire play.

The usual Stoppardian paradoxes and ironies abound. That the union hero had to become a dictator to keep his men in order is but one of these. The uncertainties that plague Stoppardian characters (his Moons) to the extent that they sometimes lose themselves in those uncertainties can be seen in the indeterminate nature of the influence that the union and government have on each other. Neither seems to succeed in its actions. The democratic ideas of freedom cannot be squared and yet maintain the original area of the circle. In fact, Stoppard seems to be reenacting the philosophical-ethical problems of George Moore and Sir Archibald Jumper (in *Jumpers*) in the political plights of Jaruzelski, Glemp, and Walesa.

Critical response to the play was divided. Sean French wrote that "it is not just the vitality of Stoppard's ideas that is exhilarating but the confidence with which he has found bizarre dramatic forms to accommodate them. He makes sophisticated use of documentary technique but it is always ironic, with a slight wink."[21] Peter Kemp, on the other hand, revived the negative criticisms of Stoppard's earlier plays, that "essentially Tom Stoppard's world is that of the under-graduate review: a brash jumble of japes, intellectual references more knowing than knowledgeable, and would-be bright ideas that—short on staying power—sputter out as merely flashy. . . . At once frivolous and dull, the play alternates between callow whimsy and boned-up bits of background."[22] Michael Church called attention to Stoppard's telling us what we already know and to the absence of suspense in the play, but described the play as "magnificent shadow-boxing" whose style lingers in the mind: "the silky music, the spare grace of the back-drops, the Busby Berkeley photography, the mass tableaux of silent figures, the acting. . . ."[23] These are all production values, of course. Church also refers briefly to the real war that had been waged over the making of the film, a war that found its way into the newspapers and into Stoppard's preface to the published play, and also a war that might itself make a play.

In this war Stoppard experienced the professional difficulty, if not the impossibility of squaring a circle. Known for his willingness to change his scripts, as in the case of the New York production of *The Real Thing*, he found himself in the role of mediator between English director Mike Hodges and the American producers. The Anglo-American marriage eventually resulted in a divorce, whose conse-quences were two different television productions of the same play. (It was the English version that won a gold award at the International Film and Television Festival in New York.)

The production and marketing of the film made almost as much news as did the play itself. In addition to production misalliances, there were the announcement and subsequent retractions in the *Times* that the film had been sold to Poland for showing in that country.

What distinguishes this political play from *Professional Foul* and other political dramas by a dramatist French describes as England's most "brilliant right-wing writer" is his use of a teaching style em-ployed by left-wing theorists such as John McGrath and Edward Bond for years. The teaching style rather than the traditional imita-tive techniques of drama seeks to convince us not that "what we are seeing is real, but that it is true." At one point, the American nar-rator (who became a point of conflict between the English director and American producers) states that "everything is true except the words and the pictures." Stoppard's earlier political plays imitate; *Squaring the Circle* shows and, therefore, teaches. Church also notes the "variegated gallery of all too human puppets. And, just once, a vintage, Left-baiting Stoppardism. 'Theory's no guarantee of social justice,' gurgled a drunkard on a swing. 'It's social justice tells you if the theory's any good.' "[24]

Chapter Twelve
Radio Plays

It is a commonplace of Stoppardian criticism that creative plagiarism of other writers is a major hallmark of his dramas. He reinvents a Philoctetes, a Willy Loman, Rosencrantz and Guildenstern, Cecily and Gwendolen, Didi and Gogo. Yet he also reinvents his own characters. The early radio plays, complete and satisfying sketches in themselves, contain especially interesting characters and situations that reappear in the long dramas.

In addition to five episodes of a radio serial, *The Dales* (1964), and seventy episodes of another serial, *A Student's Diary* (1965), Stoppard wrote more than a dozen radio and television plays, most of which have been published and/or later performed on stage. With the exception of *Professional Foul*, a television drama that is discussed in the chapter on minor stage plays because of its kinship to other political plays, these plays will be dealt with in two groups: first, the radio plays and then the television dramas.

In the very titles of his first two radio pieces, *The Dissolution of Dominic Boot* and *"M" Is for Moon Among Other Things*, two names appear that become the basis for two types of stock characters to be found in most of Stoppard's plays. These are Moon and Boot, who sometimes are combined and at other times exchange places, but much of the time remain in their separate identities. As already discussed in connection with various plays, the Moon character is one to whom things are done, and the Boot is one who takes matters into his hands and attempts to do things.

The Dissolution of Dominic Boot (1964)

In *The Dissolution of Dominic Boot*, a fifteen-minute sketch broadcast on 20 February 1964, a young upper-class dandy experiences a farcically extended taxi ride, as he tries to acquire money to pay for the ride from various friends, relatives, and banking institutions.

The taxi driver, having developed some intimacy with Dominic, even offers to buy his desk and mirror. Dominic, charming but ineffectual, takes on the qualities of a Wodehouse character caricature. He finally ends up in his office, facing his employer and dressed only in pajamas and raincoat. With stylistic aplomb, Stoppard ends the sketch with the office secretary, as she hails a taxi and calls to Dominic: "Come on, you can drop me off."

Hayman calls attention to the crisp dialogue and the skillful cutting that allow the listener to learn much about the other characters from occasional one-line comments, such as that by Dominic's father when he admonishes Bates to give a half crown to the taxi driver and bring some whiskey. The play illustrates Stoppard's basic plot technique of establishing a premise, frequently an absurd one, and allowing it to develop on its own logic. Stoppard claims this as his first original play. There is a faintly autobiographical cast to this radio play, as acquaintances remember that Stoppard was wont to ride in a taxi rather than a bus, even before his financial situation approached what it is now.

"M" Is for Moon Among Other Things (1964)

In a reference to Faber and Faber's rejection of *"M" Is for Moon Among Other Things* as a short story, Stoppard commented on the play as being about Marilyn Monroe's death. Monroe's death served for many as the end of the age of the movie sex goddess, just as Churchill's funeral seemed the end of the traditional hero in *Lord Malquist and Mr. Moon*, and the space quarrels of the lunanauts in *Jumpers* seemed to end romantic moon associations for Dotty Moore.

The opening of this second of the short radio plays, also a fifteen-minute sketch—broadcast on 6 April 1964—is a scene that can be found in Chekhov's "The Lottery Ticket," Pinter's *The Birthday Party*, or Ionesco's *The Bald Soprano*. A middle-aged and middle-class couple, who have become strangers to each other, are at home, each involved in his and her own world. As she reads an encyclopedia volume just received in the mail, he reads a newspaper and listens to television news. The non sequiturs that occur in their desultory conversation strongly suggest the dialogue between Mr. and Mrs. Smith and Mr. and Mrs. Martin of Ionesco fame. When she asks what day it is, he replies: "Mmm? . . . surging to sixty mph in twenty-nine seconds."[1] Their divergent minds converge momentarily when Alfred learns as he turns on the television set that *Dial M for Murder* is finishing and that Marilyn Monroe has just died.

Weighed down by the complex trivia of her existence, Constance comments on the simplicity of the past. Then she knew that "A is for Apple, B is for Baby, C is for Cat . . . M was for Moon."[2] In his own world, Alfred is concerned with the news of the death of Marilyn Monroe: "Marilyn . . . don't worry, I'm glad you phoned. . . ."[3] Throughout the short play, the disparate mind wanderings of the couple are indicated as "thinking," a device Stoppard employs in his writing, most noticeably in his characterization of Ruth in *Night and Day*. Like the couple in *Another Moon Called Earth*, Constance and Alfred are early Stoppardian characters who anticipate the more complex characters in later plays such as Dotty and George Moore in *Jumpers*.

Albert's Bridge (1967)

Of Stoppard's remaining radio plays—*Albert's Bridge, If You're Glad I'll Be Frank, Artist Descending a Staircase, Where Are They Now?*, and *The Dog It Was That Died*—*Albert's Bridge*, a sixty-minute drama aired on 13 July 1967, remains distinctive for several reasons.

Winner of the *Prix Italia* radio award in 1968, it was described as "an almost textbook example of what a radio play ought to be."[4] The three-part formula of this model radio play consists of "a dominant central image, a strong appeal to the visual imagination; and an action set mainly inside the head of the protagonist."[5]

Like *Lord Malquist and Mr. Moon*, *Albert's Bridge* contains stylistic devices, ideas, and even a central character that reappear in later plays. The main character, Albert, is a recent philosophy graduate whose insistence on order and perspective is a younger version of the middle-aged George Moore in *Jumpers*. Janus-faced, the play also looks back to *Enter a Free Man*, in which the prison of domesticity is the context from which George Riley attempts to extricate himself.

Albert's middle-class mother, who opposed his university education from the start, tells him that he could have been an executive trainee by now. His father, chairman of Metal Alloys and Allied Metals, reminds Albert that when he was his son's age he had six years of work behind him. The situation is aggravated by Albert's having impregnated the family maid. Feeling imprisoned by the possible domestic and intellectual situation, he rejects the expectations of his family to join the father's firm. Things come to a head when Albert decides to take a temporary job painting Clufton Bay Bridge, even as he dreams of becoming articled to a philosopher with the goal of having his "own thriving little philosopher's office in a few years."[6]

But his parents think otherwise. In a three-way conversation in which no one listens to anyone else, mother, father, and son carry on a dialogue of non sequiturs in which the dreams or concerns of each are expressed:

MOTHER:	Ring for Kate, would you, Albert?
ALBERT *(going)*:	Yes, mother.
MOTHER:	That reminds me.
FATHER:	You'll start where I started. On the shop floor.
ALBERT *(approach)*:	Well, actually, Father—
MOTHER:	I don't want to sound Victorian, but one can't just turn a blind eye.
	. . .
FATHER:	You can come in on Monday and I'll hand you over to the plant foreman.
ALBERT:	I've already got a job. Actually.
FATHER:	You haven't got a job till I give you one.
ALBERT:	I'm going to paint Clufton Bay Bridge, starting Monday.

(21)

The balance of the play shifts from scenes on the bridge, where Albert paints, to those involving his domestic life with Kate, with whom he now lives in a cramped apartment.

It is obvious in the very first scene that Albert's painting of Clufton Bay Bridge has taken on for him a poetic rhythm that is obsessive. Bob, Charlie, and Dad, his fellow workers, leave at the end of a day's work, while Albert is reluctant to go. In response to their questions, he lingers: "Right! Dip-brush-slap-slide-slick, and once again, dip, brush, slap—oh it goes on so nicely . . . tickle it into the corner, there, behind the rivet" (10). For Albert, painting is poetry, a perfect equation of time, place, and energy. The painting motions repeat themselves through this short soliloquy and, indeed, throughout the play. Rhythmic, mechanical motions are a device that

Stoppard uses later in *Dogg's Our Pet* and in *Dogg's Hamlet, Cahoot's Macbeth*, a device by which the very sound and rhythm of language create their own meaning.

Also in this first scene, Albert croons softly to himself, confusing a variety of "moon" songs:

> How high the moon in June?
> how blue the moon when it's high noon
> and the turtle doves above
> croon out of tune in love
> saying please above the trees
> which when there's thunder you don't run under
> —those trees—
> 'cos there'll be pennies fall on Alabama
> and you'll drown in foggy London town
> the sun was shi-ning . . . on my Yiddisher Mama.
>
> (9)

The many songs sung in Stoppard's plays mirror the dissolution of the conventional order and are frequently about the moon and its crumbling romance mythology.

The main action of the play concerns a decision by the local council to save money by having one person, rather than four, paint the bridge once every eight years, as it will take him that long to finish one coat, only to begin the next. His fellow workers decline the job when it is offered, and Albert, after some skepticism on the part of his employers about his ability, accepts the offer. He paints for two years and envisions being thirty when he finishes, and he can look forward to a continuity in the job and in the perspective on the chaos below him. He has, indeed, chosen, like Lord Malquist in Stoppard's novel, to withdraw from the chaos and pointlessness of existence below to a life-style of his choice. He has created his own context. Of his parents' admonitions and of their general attitudes he says: "What could they possibly know? I saw more up there in three weeks than those dots did in three years. I saw the context. It reduced philosophy and everything else. I got a perspective" (17–18).

When the council later changes its one-man painting plan, it decides on an extremely opposite one: to paint the bridge in one day with the added help of 1,799 workers, who, when they march without breaking step, cause the bridge to collapse, taking with them Albert and his friend Fraser, a would-be suicide who climbs the bridge on occasions to jump but who, when the moment comes, decides to descend, only to climb back again the next time. Fraser, perhaps, is the Sisyphus of Greek mythology, who rolls the stone to the top of the mountain, only to have it roll down and be pushed up again.

Albert's total obsession with his bridge is emphasized when Fraser first appears. He is at first a challenger and an intruder of whom Albert asks: "What are you doing on my bridge?"(31). Although the two soon form a sympathetic duo as they discuss the chaos below, each has his own means of handling it. Their difference is expressed in a Yeatsian line in one of Fraser's philosophical ruminations: "The center cannot hold . . ." (39). Later he accuses Albert of thinking only of himself as the center, "whereas I know that I am not placed at all" (39). In *Rosencrantz and Guildenstern Are Dead*, this center is frequently alluded to as the still point. As a partial Boot character, Albert is creating his center, while as a partial Moon character, Fraser has no place. Fraser's means of coping is to climb up and then down the bridge, rather than staying as Albert does.

Attempting to free himself from the enormity of the disorder below, Fraser climbs the bridge intending to commit suicide, but changes his mind when he finds "the idea of society is just about tenable" (34) from the height of the bridge. He sees the semblance of patterns in the one-way streets and "supply meeting demand," but also realizes that "somewhere there is a lynch pin, which, when removed, will collapse the whole monkey-puzzle" (32). His comment is prophetic of the bridge collapse at the end of the play. Fraser is the victim of the chaos around him and reminds one of Moon in Stoppard's novel, a character who carries a ticking bomb throughout that work. To Fraser, "the city is a hold in which blind prisoners are packed wall to wall. Motor-cars nose each other down every street, and they are beginning to breed, spread. . . . There's too much of everything, but the space for it is constant. So the shell of human existence is filling out, expanding, and it's going to go bang"(31–32).

Moon's bomb explodes at the end of the novel, and Albert's bridge collapses, killing those aboard.

Stoppard's central image of the bridge as dominant metaphor is a device effectively used by earlier dramatists such as Ibsen in *The Wild Duck*, Chekhov in *The Cherry Orchard*, and Tennessee Williams in *The Glass Menagerie*. In each of these dramas, the sense of dissolution pertains, and the metaphor affords opportunity for the exploration of diverse attitudes toward the one image of order in a dissolving world. As Irving Wardle points out in his review, the bridge represents a wasted life to the old workman, a challenge to the efficiency expert, a family memorial to the council chairman, and a chance in applied philosophy to Albert, whose connection to himself and the world breaks with the collapse.[7] Albert is the new hero who experiences the chaos of the times and chooses his context as an alternative to that provided for him by parents, wife, and child, and, indeed, his very education.

Finally, the play contains possible autobiographical references, rare though these are in Stoppard's writing: Albert's father heads a large industrial firm, while Stoppard's stepfather climbed the ladder of the machine tool business on his return to England from India. And in his medley of songs at the beginning Albert inserts "the sun was shining . . . on my Yiddisher Mama" (9); in his profile of Stoppard, Kenneth Tynan refers to the fact that either Eugene or Martha Straussler had at least one parent of Jewish descent. Stoppard, unlike Albert, bypassed university education, choosing instead to become a reporter. As a reporter in Bristol, however, he made friends at the university and read much, educating himself. His rendering of the logical positivists in *Jumpers* demonstrates an impressive knowledge of philosophy.

If You're Glad I'll Be Frank (1966)

Referred to frequently as one of Stoppard's most Ionesco-like plays, *If You're Glad I'll Be Frank*, a thirty-minute piece aired on BBC Radio 8 February 1966, treats two characters, husband and wife, who have lost control of their lives, indeed lost track of each other. In Ionesco's plays people are constantly metamorphosed into animals and objects by the pressures of modern life, as in *The Rhinoceros* and *The Tenant*. In Stoppard's plays, however, fantasy takes over at the point at which people in Ionesco's plays are destroyed.

In this radio drama, two of the most repetitive careers in modern society are represented in bus driving and telephone services. Frank, a bus driver, one day recognizes his lost wife's voice when he dials "TIM" (a dial-a-time service provided by Telephone Services). Excitedly he begins a long and confusing search for his wife, Gladys. As

Glad reveals in one of her interior monologues, they had met dancing, when he had said to her, "If you're Glad I'll be Frank." She remembers those days as a "time to laugh then but while I laughed a bumble-bee fluttered its wings a million times" (57). She found herself unable to compete with his bus route during which he passed her window twice a day, "with a toot and a wave and was gone." "He took his timetable seriously" (57). Her earlier disappointment in life at not being accepted into a convent where she expected to find peace only made her want to "sneeze the fear of God into their alarm-setting, egg-timing, train-catching, coffee-breaking faith in an uncomprehending clock work" (62).

Passengers on Frank's bus riot when they are delayed as a result of Frank's bursting into the Telephone Services office one day, demanding to know what they (post office bureaucrats) have done with his wife. His demands are confused by Sir John (First Lord of the Post Office) with possible innuendos about his own marital infidelities. Outside the office the noise of the rioting passengers is like that of the 1,800 marching men in *Albert's Bridge*. A collapse similar to that of the bridge occurs when Gladys misses the beats in her time announcements. Her disruption is reported by the secretary Miss Bligh (a name used in *The Dissolution of Dominic Boot*). Gladys, sobbing hysterically, doesn't know and doesn't care what time it is, "because it doesn't go tick tock at all, it just goes and I have seen—I have seen infinity!" (69). Her comment is similar to one Duncan McFee makes to Crouch in *Jumpers*: "I have seen the future, Henry, . . . and it's yellow" (*Jumpers*, 80). This crisis point in Gladys' life is similar to that undergone by other characters of Stoppard. When Gladys hears the soothing voice of the First Lord urging her to pull herself together and get back on the rails, she does. The last words of the play are those of the speaking clock, TIM, repeating the time, punctuated only by the "pip, pip, pips."

Using time both as subject matter and as a stylistic device to maintain a spoken rhythm, Stoppard has created a "real theatrical Fabergé, juggling excellent but straightforward jokes . . . with a constant stream of time-metaphors turned inside out, all spinning round the still human centre of Gladys, from whom we hear both the tones of TIM and her own interior monologue."[8]

Stoppard's time gymnastics are achieved by inserting Gladys's time announcements and her personalized reveries into the actual time spans of seconds between the announcements and the pips. The effect is a perfect timing, as perfect as that of the physical gymnastics, so effectively realized in *Jumpers*. The combination of time as structure, with its repetitively accurate nature, with that of time as subject is a phenomenal juggling act. As subject, time in the image of the speaking clock is the means by which Gladys can contain the chaos of her personal life. The clock job provides her with the peace of monotonous regularity that the convent earlier had denied her. The clock to her is what the bridge is to Albert.

In some of her reveries contained within the split-second timing of the speaking clock, TIM, she indulges in poetic soliloquies that suggest the very illusory nature of time, and, indeed, of life itself:

> And if I stopped to explain
> At the third stroke it will be
> too late to catch up, far
> far too late, gentlemen. . . .
> they'd complain, to the Post Office
> And if stopped altogether,
> just stopped, gave up the pretence,
> it would make no difference.
> Silence is the sound of time passing.
> (55–56)

Gladys realizes that there is no pendulum that swings. There is only the clock that goes tick tock, and never the time that chimes or that stops. She, indeed, has seen infinity, as she asserts.

The central images in Stoppard's dramas take on a rich variety, from George Riley's reusable envelope, Lord Malquist's chosen anachronistic eighteenth-century life-style, and Albert's bridge to Gladys's speaking clock. The images as metaphors grow profusely in his subsequent plays.

Sometimes the images are verbal rather than visual, such as the Dogg language of the schoolboys in *Dogg's Our Pet*, a playful device that turns deadly serious in *Cahoot's Macbeth*. Some of this verbal play rhythmically expresses Gladys's security in regularity:

> Check, check, check. . . .
> One day I'll give him something
> to check up for . . .
> tick tock
> tick tock

> check check
> chick chock
> tick
> you can check
> your click clock
> by my pip pip pip
>
> (60)

Ronald Hayman calls attention to the influence of T. S. Eliot in Gladys's rhythmic time-announcements, particularly to the constructions of her reveries as they suggest the verse structures in *The Four Quartets* and the choric uncles and aunts of *The Family Reunion*.[9]

Artist Descending a Staircase (1972)

First aired on BBC Radio 3 on 14 November 1972, *Artist Descending a Staircase*, a sixty-minute radio play, has been seen by critics as a forerunner of *Travesties*, Stoppard's full-length play about artists and revolutions. In the radio play there are three artists: Beauchamp, a tonal artist who experiments with sounds on tape; Donner, who paints; and Martello, who sculpts. Similarly in *Travesties* there are three characters—Lenin, Joyce, and Tzara—who argue about the nature and purpose of art, and who represent revolutions in politics, literature, and art.

Again Stoppard's penchant for sources is the basis for the situations of *Artist Descending a Staircase*, the source this time being the artist Marcel Duchamp, and, in particular, his painting *Nude Descending a Staircase*. Like the changing images of Duchamp's nude as she descends the staircase, the perspectives of the three main characters shift in Stoppard's play. Extending Duchamp's image of the descending nude, the author uses the staircase descents of two characters who fall to their deaths as the plot machinery or, in his own words, the nuts and bolts of the drama.

In fact, the very arrangement of the eleven scenes of the play is one of descent and ascent, described by Hayman as a V.[10] Having executed an ingenious use of time in *Albert's Bridge*, Stoppard invents still another here.

Moving from the present back to 1914 and then in a reversal back to the present, he depicts the lives of three communal artists in eleven scenes, the sixth of which takes place in 1914. As a result, the time frames of scenes 1 and 11 are similar, as are those of 2 and 10,

3 and 9, 4 and 8, and 5 and 7. Because radio can provide the necessary fluidity that the stage cannot give, the time sequence is highly
successful. In fact, when Harold Pinter's *Betrayal*, which deploys a
linear backward time sequence, was produced on the screen, its reception was generally more favorable than that of the stage performance, which somehow seemed awkward and, perhaps, even gimmicky.

In the very first scene Beauchamp and Martello, now old, accuse
each other of the death of their quarrelsome friend Donner, also old.
They are listening to a tape, one of Beauchamp's experiments in tonal
art, of the noises recorded during the fall of Donner to his death. The
sequence of sounds includes an irregular droning, stealthy footsteps,
a creaking board, the stopping of the droning and creaking, Donner's
exclamation: "Ah! There you are," two more quick steps, a thump
and then Donner's cry as he falls.

As the action moves backward in time, the audience learns of
Beauchamp's meeting Sophie Farthingale, a nearly blind schoolgirl,
on a park bench. She is not sure, when she becomes totally blind,
which of the three artists she had fallen in love with when she had
seen them posing for a photographer, each in front of one of his
paintings. After her vague descriptions of a snow scene with a fence,
Donner decided that the painting belonged to Beauchamp. So it is he
on whom Sophie settles.

Uncertain about her status in the quarters occupied by the three
men, uncertainty made more urgent by her increasing blindness, Sophie decides she can't tolerate being watched, moving about the
room, "grieving, talking to myself, sleeping, washing, dressing, un-
dressing, crying" (112). Next we hear the sound of smashing wood
and glass and then the sound of her body hitting the floor. Preceding
her death, footsteps are heard descending the staircase. The coroner
calls her death a "tragic defenestration" (112). Martello sees her
death, in an ironic twist, as an event that might have killed Donner,
had she fallen a yard to her right. Donner, who has been in love with
Sophie all along, is painting her portrait.

The last scene repeats the tape heard at the opening. As Beauchamp and Martello listen, still discussing what to do with Donner's
body, they are distracted by a droning fly in the room. Indeed, the
noise turns out to be the same as that on the tape. Both men realize
that Donner's "Ah! There you are," had been addressed to the fly he
had attempted to swat when he fell to his death. The play closes with
a short laugh from Beauchamp as he recites Gloucester's Lines from

King Lear: " 'As flies to wanton boys are we to the Gods: they kill us for their sport.' Now then" (116).

The line from Shakespeare effectively rounds off the Beckettian touches at the beginning and end, in which the tape listening suggests the old man of *Krapp's Last Tape* reliving memorable moments of his life as he listens to a recording. Acknowledged influences on Stoppard, both Shakespeare and Beckett influence this radio drama, just as in a more complex manner they provide Stoppard with style and substance for *Rosencrantz and Guildenstern Are Dead.* The parodic use of the *King Lear* lines trivializes an already trivial, aging, second-rate artist. Similarly, the parodic adaptation of the tape-listening device in its sordid context contrasts sharply with the original version in which Krapp listens with sensuous pleasure to the recording of early experiences that are only heightened in the remembering. Stoppard's joke playing here is effective, its parody totally contained in the recurrent image of the fly.

Within the movements in time, backward and forward, in the various scenes of the play, there is the usual Stoppardian debate of ideas, handled not as brilliantly as in *Jumpers* or *Travesties*, but in keeping with the mediocrity of the artists and their blurred visions in old age, recalling the banal and limited views of Carr in *Travesties*.

The cognomen syndrome serves handily to express this second-rate quality. At one point Beauchamp recalls that in Zurich in 1915 Tarzan was too conservative. Attempting to correct him, Donner counters with "Tsar Nicholas?" It is not until Donner remembers "Hugo Ball and Hans Arp Max, Kurt, André . . . Picabia . . . Tristan Tzara" (86) that Beauchamp recognizes the right name, Tzara. Tzara, of course, is one of the three revolutionaries in *Travesties*. Stoppard's joking on the dadaists grows in ludicrousness when Martello projects a sculpture called "The Cripple" in which the figure would be a "wooden man with a real leg." Sophie responds with her suggestion of a "black-patch-man with a real eye" (94).

There is much debating about art in the play. Martello questions naturalistic art, contending that the "greater the success, the more false the result. It is only when the imagination is dragged away from what the eye sees that a picture becomes interesting" (101). He describes the painting of a perfect apple as a technique anyone can learn, like playing the piano. "But how can you teach someone to *think* in a certain way?—to paint an utterly simple shape in order to ambush the mind with something quite unexpected about that shape by hanging it in a frame and forcing you to see it, as it were, for the first time" (101).

The debates about artistic theories are contained within the plot mechanism revolving around the death of Donner, as the two surviving artists accuse each other of his staircase-descending death. The parody of the shifting perspectives in the famous Duchamp painting trivializes Stoppard's three mediocre artists. Compounding the trivialization is Stoppard's ambush for the audience in the image of the buzzing fly as the possible explanation for the death of Donner. As with Carr in *Travesties*, Stoppard's use of the artists as old men with blurred vision deflates audience expectations regarding a possible murder and does so with perfect credibility. Stoppard's parody of the title of Duchamp's painting embraces the two literal descents that result in deaths and the two shifts in perspectives regarding the object of Sophie's love and the cause of Donner's death.

Where Are They Now? (1970)

"Whither Mr. Chips," quips one of a group of old boys at a public school reunion dinner. A journalist of some repute by the name of Gale, nicknamed Groucho during his school days, launches a scathing attack on one of England's staunchest institutions in *Where Are They Now?*, Stoppard's contribution to a long list of British plays about schoolboys and schoolmasters. Commissioned for BBC's School Radio, the play was first broadcast on 28 January 1970 and then rebroadcast on BBC Radio 3 on 18 December 1970.

Like the two radio plays just discussed, *Where Are They Now?* experiments successfully with still another time structure. The years 1945 and 1969 are the alternating time frames within which the action of the nine scenes occurs. Although the scenes alternate in time, the author makes it clear in the stage directions that they be played as continuous rather than alternate years. The strategy works, since the old schoolboys are treated by their old schoolmaster, Dobson, much as in their youth twenty-five years ago. The intractable continuity of public school traditions is emphasized by the insistence on continuous scene sequence.

But underneath the surface, discontinuity rears its head in the character of the dissonant Gale, who, while the headmaster talks, engages in a running commentary to those at his table about the brutality of pedagogical techniques. "We walked into French like condemned men. We were too afraid to *learn*. All our energy went into ingratiating ourselves and deflecting his sadism on to our friends. We brought him lumps of French to propitiate him until the bell went, and some of it stuck . . ." (135). A crusading journalist, Gale is the only old boy present about whose career Dobson, the old schoolmaster at the same table, was unsure, since Gale had failed to contribute to the school magazine's *"Where Are They Now?"* page.

A usurper at the reunion, Jenkins by mistake occupies a seat reserved for another Jenkins, the French master whom Gale criticizes and whom Gale had asked to be seated at his table, not realizing that he (Jenkins) had died. The intruder Jenkins mistakenly crashes this dinner. The mistake is partly due to the change of the meeting room, the first ever, from the downstairs to the upstairs dining hall. The intruder belongs downstairs where a reunion is being held by the Oakleigh House for the Sons of Merchant Seamen's Widows.

Ironically, it is Jenkins who remembers his school days with an emotional sincerity, a sharp contrast with Gale's cynical view of the old days. For Jenkins "the old school *was* my England . . . at least it was the part I knew best and thought about, and missed. I had a fine time . . . good friends. We all seemed to belong to each other, you know. Do you know what I mean?" (130–31).

Gale replies quietly: "No." He wishes "there was a way to let small boys know that it doesn't really matter. I wish I could give them the scorn to ride them out—those momentous trivialities and tiny desolations" (136–37). Of his French master, Gale says that he taught nothing but fear. Another old boy, Marks, Harpo to Gale's Groucho during their school days, merely comments: "Trust Groucho to make a scene" (135).

Traditions run deep, and at the reunion schoolboy nicknames are resumed. Gale, Brindley, and Marks are Groucho, Chico, and Harpo, respectively. The tradition of complaining about the cheap wine at dinner echoes their complaining about the food in earlier days. The continuity is most pointedly depicted in the presence of a very recent graduate, Crawford, who in one of the contemporary scenes is shown harshly treating Marks's young son, presently enrolled at the school. The only thing that has changed in the twenty-five years is the location of the room in which the dinner is held.

Again in this play about schoolboys, Stoppard uses a second language—that of the schoolboy—in the scenes involving the young boys. "Mog, chit, frits, Staggers, tunky, frogspawn, wocs" are words whose sound and rhythmic usage convey meanings known only to the boys. In this radio play, they are part of the traditions of the public school. As stated earlier, the device as used in *Cahoot's Macbeth* becomes a means of survival in a world where traditional language has been corrupted into tyranny. In public schools, the language games are just that.

One of Stoppard's rare autobiographical references occurs in the main character, Gale, who is a reporter as Stoppard was. And like Stoppard he is disillusioned about the school system, in particular, about the sadism that prevents real learning. Stoppard has told interviewers of his dislike of school and of his selling all of his books as a youth. He has spoken of being conscious of his foreign accent as a schoolboy, so that Gale's criticism, muttered at a crucial moment at the reunion dinner, might well be Stoppard's own.

Like the other radio plays discussed, *Where Are They Now?* contains still another experiment with time as structure, in this case, the contiguous rendering of two periods, twenty-five years apart in real life.

The Dog It Was That Died (1982)

Having parodied Agatha Christie in *The Real Inspector Hound* and having made a mysterious murder a part of many of his dramas as in *Artist Descending a Staircase, Another Moon Called Earth,* and *Jumpers*, Stoppard once more ingeniously parodies the double agent plot of Le Carré in *The Dog It Was That Died*. Broadcast on BBC Radio in 1982, the drama is included in a collected volume (1983) that contains previously unpublished earlier radio and television works: *The Dissolution of Dominic Boot, "M" Is for Moon Among Other Things* (radio); *Teeth, Another Moon Called Earth,* and *Neutral Ground* (television). Also included in the volume is the television piece *A Separate Peace,* which had previously been published in a Grove Press collection.

In *The Dog It Was That Died*, Stoppard returns to a form, the radio play, that he had written in the sixties. About twenty years later, he wrote his sixth radio play, this time about a double agent named Purvis who was shuffled so much between Gell, his British contact, and Rashnikov, his Soviet contact, that he became, in his own words, a canister, a set of Russian dolls (only the last of which is not hollow), and, indeed, a hollow man. This last self-identification once more reflects the touch of T. S. Eliot so strong in Stoppard's early writing, particularly *Lord Malquist and Mr. Moon*.

The action of the play involves Purvis's attempted suicide from Chelsea Bridge. Instead of drowning, however, he lands on a barge, killing a dog. He is then sent to Clifftops, a place where burned out agents are sent for treatment. Visited by his superior, Blair, he is killed when his wheelchair rolls off a cliff. Whether the accident is really that or whether Blair pushed the wheelchair is, as in *Jumpers* and other plays, left to the audience. Perfectly rational explanations for either case are provided by the author.

Between the suicide attempt at the beginning and the death at the end, the reader is provided with arguments on both sides. Purvis writes letters that specify malfeasance, such as opium dens and sexual acts, involving his superiors, who then would wish to be rid of him. They later, however, explain these actions away. There is also some doubt about Purvis's loyalty. And it is on this latter point that the real discussion and argument hinge. Yet it is not the skepticism of his superiors but Purvis's self-knowledge that devastates him so. Truths, lies, countertruths, and counterlies become so interchangeable that they lose all meaning. Describing himself as a loyal patriot who hated foreigners, Purvis soon found his idealism vanishing as both sides fed him instructions to make the opposite side feel he was working for *it*, until his own opinions just got lost.

Purvis uses a simple personal experience to illustrate a point. Once a friend called him to ask if they should meet at the Savoy or Simpson's. In an attempt to be flexible, one suggests the meeting at Simpson's or, perhaps, the Savoy, and the other agrees and sets the time at 8:30 and then hangs up. Is it the Savoy or Simpson's, then? So with Purvis and his counterintelligence work. The discussions with his Soviet contacts left him with ideas such as historical inevitability and worker power that seemed as natural as ideas of democracy, free expression, free market forces, etc. Gell and Rashnikov between them had reduced Purvis to a canister, a hollow man. Ideas in the double agent's life are reduced to words and words to nothing. Both agent and words are hollow.

Like *Every Good Boy Deserves Favour, The Dog It Was That Died* deals with the reduction of man to a cipher. The insanity takes on a logic of its own. Like *Neutral Ground*, broadcast in 1968, *The Dog It Was That Died* deals with the neutralization process; in the earlier play an agent is stranded in a no-man's land, left without a country; in the later play he is left without an identity. Language and ideas are stranded, left without meaning. The play's title is, indeed, effectively ambiguous.

Faber's 1983 collection of radio and television plays appropriately begins with *The Dog It Was That Died* and ends with *Neutral Ground*, both spy tales. In them, Sophocles and Le Carré, respectively, have been ingeniously parodied. Stoppard remains a master parodist in these two spy tales about victims who are Moon characters to whom things are done.

Chapter Thirteen
Television Plays

Stoppard's first television play, *A Walk on the Water*, was aired on British Independent Television in 1963. Revised and retitled *Enter a Free Man*, it opened as a stage play in 1968, after *Rosencrantz and Guildenstern Are Dead* had made history at Cranston Hall, Edinburgh, during the Festival of 1966 and at the Old Vic in 1967. Discussed in another chapter, it is noted here simply as the first of a series of television plays by Stoppard.

On the whole, the television pieces lack the stylistic distinctiveness of radio plays, such as *Albert's Bridge*, *If You're Glad I'll Be Frank*, and *Artist Descending a Staircase*, in which time functions ingeniously as substance and structure.

Stoppard expressed his views on writing for film, in particular, the television film, *The Engagement*, shown on NBC in the United States: ". . . things on television have to last a certain time, like 51 minutes and 48 seconds, which is kind of absurd to somebody who has worked mainly in the theater. . . . A play is something which happens behind closed doors between consenting adults; and a film is a kind of three-ring circus, and the director is the elephant act, and the writer is a sort of clod who comes on afterwards and cleans up the mess."[1]

A Separate Peace

The main character of *A Separate Peace* is John Brown, who appears one morning at 2:30 A.M. at the office of the Beechwood Nursing Home, "a biggish man in his late forties, with a well-lined face; calm pleasant, implacable,"[2] carrying two zipped grips. He is pleased by the "neatness, the quiet, the flowers, the nice nurse . . ." (143). Although not ill, he insists on being admitted to the hospital, claiming he is an emergency patient. Adamant about abiding by regulations, he wants to pay in advance and goes through all the motions of admission, against the protests of the nurse and doctor on duty. When the nurse accidentally opens one suitcase full of bank notes, she and

the doctor decide to humor him while they investigate, much the
same way George Riley is humored by his pub companions in *Enter
a Free Man*.

Brown is still another version of the Stoppardian character who sees
the chaos around him and chooses to withdraw from that chaos in
order to create his own context. Having found peace as a child patient
at Beechwood and then later in a prisoner-of-war camp, he has for a
brief time found it again at the hospital. Speaking of his four years
in a prison camp, he confides to Maggie:

> Yes. . . . Funny thing, that camp. Up to then it was all terrible. Chaos—
> all the pins must have fallen off the map. The queue on the beach—dive
> bombers and bullets. Oh dear, yes. The camp was like breathing-out for the
> first time in months. I couldn't believe it. It was like winning, being cap-
> tured. . . . The war was still going on but I wasn't going to it any more.
> They gave us food, life was regulated, in a box of earth and wire and sky,
> and sometimes you'd hear an aeroplane miles up, but it couldn't touch you.
> On my second day I knew what it reminded me of. (168)

Asked by Maggie what it reminded him of, Brown responds: "Here.
It reminded me of here" (169).

In his many conversations with Maggie, during which he talked
about his postwar years, he spoke of the way the peace didn't match
up to the war. He fancied being a lighthouse keeper, but that didn't
work out. He thought of being a monk, but there was no "monastery
for agnostics" (170). Finally he settled for, in Maggie's words, a
"hospital for the healthy" (170).

Brown's farewell words to Maggie illustrate Stoppard's device of
creating an illogical or abnormal situation and then proceeding with
a logic that is irrefutable: "Trouble is, I've always been so *well*. If I'd
been *sick* I would have been all right" (174). This inversion of the
normal state of things is the source of much quiet, whimsical humor
throughout the play. It is especially strong in the dialogue carried on
between Brown and the doctor at first and then later between Brown
and the Matron:

> MATRON: We have to keep the beds free for people who need them.
>
> BROWN: I need this room.
>
> MATRON: I believe you, Mr. Brown—but wouldn't another room like
> this one do?—somewhere else? You see, we deal with phys-
> ical matters—of the body—

BROWN: There's nothing wrong with my *mind*. You won't find my name on any list. (153)

Earlier Brown confuses and puts on the defensive the nurse and doctor who interrogated him initially:

NURSE: Mr. Brown says there's nothing wrong with him.

BROWN: That's right—I—

NURSE: He just wants a bed.

BROWN: A room.

DOCTOR: But this isn't a hotel.

BROWN: Exactly.

DOCTOR: Exactly what?

BROWN: I don't follow you.

DOCTOR: Perhaps I'm confused. You see, I was asleep. (146)

When asked if he had tried the pubs in town, Brown counters with "I'm not drunk." When told that pubs have rooms, he responds, "I've got a room. What's the matter?" (147). His logic baffles theirs, and he wins out for the time being, at least.

There is a quiet humor in Brown's slowly drawing the hospital staff into his own context. Once he has been admitted, he defines his own terms and makes his impact on the place. For example, the subtle inversion of the normal hospital routine is evident in the confidentiality Maggie attempts to establish with him in order to find out more about his circumstances. It is Brown, however, who first draws out Maggie to speak of her childhood and her choice of a nursing career. Questioner, she becomes the questioned. Only then does Brown divulge the events leading up to his arrival at the hospital. Temporarily he is a Boot character who is determining his life rather than falling victim. Eventually he leaves, but even then it is in his way.

Other authors have dealt with characters like Brown. Melville's Bartleby separates himself from the normal world with his insistent "I prefer not to." Gogol's Akaky Akakyevich, whose name in Russia is as anonymous as Brown's in England, has withdrawn from life except for his scrivening. All crave the anonymity realized only in a self-chosen regulated order of things.

Closer to the situation of Stoppard's Brown, perhaps, is the narrator of the novel *A Separate Peace*, by John Knowles. Published in 1959, seven years prior to the television transmission of Stoppard's play, the novel deals with a private war the main character engages in within the context of the larger war fought in 1942. But the private conflict occurs within the safe confines of one of New England's most beautiful and harmonious private schools, insulated from the public events of the time. Fifteen years later, the narrator returns to that campus to discover whether or not he had, even unknowingly, achieved a harmony within himself, retracing his steps over familiar youthful haunts. Although Knowles's hero is developed with a psychological complexity absent in Stoppard's Brown, both men have made their peace within a World War II context.

The conventional time sequence of Stoppard's plot and the passive nature of the language express these very qualities in the character of Brown, in stark contrast to the vivid spectacles and the linguistic dazzle of Stoppard's other writing. But the hero as stylist of his life remains, as does the author's love of a contradictory process in which an illogical assumption or situation develops a logicality of its own.

Teeth (1967)

If *Where Are They Now?* is the Stoppardian version of the *Goodbye, Mr. Chips* genre, *Teeth* can be seen as his variation of still another English genre, so consummately realized in Coward's *Private Lives*, a comedy whose structural premise is the switching of marital mates by two couples.

Harry, a dentist, seeks revenge on George, the husband of his receptionist, Prudence. George has seduced Harry's wife, Mary. When George appears for a dental appointment, a psychological duel follows. Harry, with his dental equipment and with his patient in the chair, manipulates the conversation and the situation in general. Already the Boot (victimizer) and Moon (victim) characters are obvious. As Boot, Harry removes one of George's teeth, stains another with a green liquid, and, after flirting with Prudence in the presence of his helpless victim, asks George's permission to keep Prudence late that day.

The situation provides Stoppard with plenty of opportunity to exercise his verbal agility. Hayman calls attention to the many double entendres, the ambiguities, and the sophisticated technique of withholding information by Harry to test George's capacity for invention, particularly in explaining how Prudence came home wearing Mary's shoes one day. Hayman also comments on the compatibility of the thirty-minute play to the medium of television, in the many effective closeups of the patient's face as he reacts emotionally to both the dental procedures and the personal revenge attempts.[3]

Another Moon Called Earth (1967)

Perhaps no other short piece by Stoppard for stage, radio, or television seems so much a blueprint for another play as *Another Moon Called Earth* does for *Jumpers*.

Aired on BBC TV on 28 June 1967, its characters and situations are the basis for *Jumpers*. In both dramas, history-making events undermine long held certitudes. In one single public event, the world changes, and the impact of that change incapacitates the heroine while the hero attempts an explanation of events by seeking patterns of cause and effect in the history of the world.

The central characters are a married couple, Bone and Penelope. He is trying to write his history, while Penelope is obsessed with a moon landing and the consequent traumatic shift in her perspective on life. She copes only by going to bed. Like John Brown earlier, she becomes a patient, although she is not physically ill. One of her visitors is Albert, a doctor (?), who announces that she is unable to leave her bed. The circumstances of his visit suggest but do not strongly support an interest other than health. His shoes have been removed (a detail from *Teeth*). Stoppard keeps suspense in the play by confusing the spectator with "a rich mixture of evidence that suggests adultery and explanations that almost quell his (the husband's) suspicions."[4] When the doctor leaves, Bone finds Penelope at the window, watching the parade celebrating the return of the astronauts.

In both *Another Moon Called Earth* and *Jumpers*, there are domestic arguments with hints of suspected infidelity. In both, the arguments move on to conversation about the impact of the moon landing on personal attitudes. Both men, Bone and George, seem unconcerned about the impact, whereas both women, Penelope and Dotty, are emotionally affected. For Penelope the absolutes of good and evil have suddenly deteriorated into nothing more than local customs. The astronaut has smashed the mirror and has "stood outside and seen us whole, all in one go, little."[5] Penelope's paralysis caused by the moon landing is the precursor of Dotty's inability to sing her moon songs in *Jumpers*. Her reaction is also reminiscent of Gladys's glimpsing of eternity in *If You're Glad I'll be Frank* and of McFee's vision of the future as yellow in *Jumpers*.

As author (Bone) and as academic competitor (George Moore), both characters are interested in writing about the causality and interrelationship of events in an attempt to discover patterns and to expose the fallacy of chance. They are proponents of traditional systems of thought and oppose the jumperism of relativists.

Like other of Stoppard's plays, *Another Moon Called Earth* has its complement of a murder mystery or, at least, the suggestion of one. Penelope's nurse fell or was pushed from a window (recalling the similar death of Sophie in *Artist Descending a Staircase*). Professor Duncan McFee, Moore's academic rival, was shot from the pyramid of gymnasts. Murders in the plays go unsolved or unpunished. Or they are explained away as though they are the usual order of things.

Bone finds in his search for patterns causes "spreading, making connections back, wider and deeper all the time . . . [in] a sequence going back to Babylon."[6] Like Moon and Moore he is overwhelmed by the backward connections. In their attempts to understand and thereby to control, all three are Boots. In their comical failure to do so, they are Moons.

Neutral Ground (1968)

Much of the recent criticism of Stoppard's drama is concerned with his transformation into a dramatist with serious commitments. His dramas of the late seventies—*Every Good Boy Deserves Favour, Dogg's Hamlet, Cahoot's Macbeth,* and *Professional Foul*—are the basis for what has been viewed as a change in his dramatic direction. The change was reinforced by his visits to the Soviet Union and Czechoslovakia, his interests in two Czech dramatists, Vaclav Havel and Pavel Kohout, and his articles in various newspapers about the matter of artistic freedom in Eastern bloc countries.

Yet the television drama *Neutral Ground*, produced by Granada and aired on ITV about ten years earlier, concerns the tyranny in a middle European country adjoining Austria, suggesting, of course, Stoppard's native country, Czechoslovakia. Although the spy story takes precedence over direct comment on human rights, the play is about private and national conscience. Private emotions and public morality battle with each other in much the same way they do in *Professional*

Foul. Neutral Ground is Stoppard's contemporary adaptation of Sophocles' *Philoctetes*.

The hero, Philo, finds himself stranded in a country that has lost its borders and is virtually nonexistent. After fifteen years as a British spy, he is judged a bad security risk and left in this homeland without an identity. Later, British Intelligence, reversing its decision, dispatches Otis (Odysseus of Greek myth) and Acheson (Neoptolemus of Greek fame) to persuade him to return. Acheson succeeds in his persuasion, but only after a series of disillusioning experiences.

In the Greek story, Philoctetes was given Hercules' bow and arrow when he lighted Hercules' funeral pyre. Later, on the way to Troy he was bitten by a snake and left by the Greeks on the isle of Lemnos. When things weren't going well for the Greeks, Philoctetes was called on. Odysseus, the opportunist, was unable to convince him to return, but Neoptolemus, the famous son of an even more famous father, Achilles, persuaded Philoctetes to rejoin the Greek army. With his famous bow and arrow, he wounded Paris, and, although Paris's death did not crucially influence the war, the importance of the episode lies in its emphasis on the personal aspects of political action.

In the Greek tale, the personal honesty of Philoctetes and Neoptolemus is sharply contrasted with the political cunning of Odysseus. So in Stoppard's drama, the integrity of Philo and Acheson is opposite the cold, political nature of Otis. Complicating Philo's decision to return or not is his homesickness for the trees, the people, and the streets of his tyrannized homeland. Only when he jumps on to the moving train at the last moment (to save Acheson complications when he returns to England) does he make the choice.

Neutral Ground is significant as Stoppard's first dramatization of the politics of his homeland. In addition to the moral contest, there is a strongly emotional one within Philo. Indeed, as Hayman points out, Stoppard with his antiautobiographical bias never used the line "England isn't my country, you know" until he wrote "an ephemeral television thriller."[7] The charges made by critics about the lack of conscience and emotion in his major dramas and in the shorter nuts-and-bolts plays cannot be made against *Neutral Ground*.

The topicality of Stoppard's subject matter has continued since World War II, when spies, frequently former Nazis, were temporarily or permanently shelved and left without identity. On 10 January 1984, the *New York Times* ran an article on the subject, mentioning

Klaus Barbie, perhaps the most famous of such counterspies. The article mentions "that at least 1000 Nazi criminals are living in Canada, sent years ago by British and United States secret services 'to warehouse' for future use."[8]

In his review, Michael Billington referred to Stoppard's "Sophoclean spy tale" in which the author managed to "unearth a situation that had not already been done to death" in a time of an "enormous number of films and books" about espionage. Billington expressed pleasure "in seeing an effective, Le Carré-like situation exploited both for its moral content and its human values."[9]

The Engagement (1970)

Shown in the United States on NBC's "Experiment in Television" series, The Engagement is a longer version of Stoppard's earlier radio play, The Dissolution of Dominic Boot. Expanded from a fifteen-minute script into a television drama that "had to last 51 minutes and 48 seconds," the project, according to Stoppard, was frightening, since "the writer hasn't even got a sort of casting vote."[10] His friend Paul Joyce had finally succeeded, after three years, in persuading Stoppard to make the television adaptation.

The outline of the original story remains intact. The complications of Dominic's financial plight, caused by his purchase of an engagement ring for Vivian, lead him into selling nearly everything he owns in order to pay for a taxi ride, whose cost grows with every stop he makes in increasingly desperate attempts to collect money for the ride. The addition of ten attractive female office workers who collect enough money to buy him a tasteless ornament as an engagement present, and the selling of his blood for thirty shillings are only some of the episodes added to the already farcical plot. The result of the additions was to diminish the subtlety. Had the expansion involved a thirty-minute rather than a fifty-minute script, the result would have been better.[11]

Stoppard's experimentations with time in the radio plays and his employment of effective visual images in the television plays result in self-sustaining dramas, but these dramas are also important as precursors of his major stage dramas. Although the radio and television plays were written and aired mostly in his early career, they are a part of his later writing years, as Professional Foul (1977) and Squaring the Circle (1984) demonstrate.[12]

Chapter Fourteen
Stage Adaptations and Screenplays

Adaptations

"The whole knack of adaptation—you're faced with many alternatives but only one choice is right. *That's* the abstract idea of translation I suppose. The problems one faces with translations is the more free you get the more natural it sounds. The more literal the less natural. These two lines have to come to some sort of a deal. You have to find out where to cross the freedom line, where the fidelity line. Another danger is that you actually can iron out inflection and phrases which make the situation Spanish. You fall into a trap and it all slides off into a kind of 'Knightsbridge.' "[1]

These comments by Stoppard in an interview for *Plays and Players* in regard to his adaptation of Lorca's *The House of Bernarda Alba* contain the dilemma translators in general experience as they maneuver their ways between close fidelity to the original and fidelity to their understanding of the meaning and spirit of that original. Increasingly successful with every attempt, Stoppard has adapted five dramas, four of which are central eastern European in origin and one Spanish. He has worked from literal translations, as well as with persons familiar with those languages he does not know. Thus he has judiciously approached the fidelity and freedom lines to avoid the "Knightsbridge" trap.

His stage adaptations include Slawomir Mrozek's *Tango*, Lorca's *The House of Bernarda Alba*, Schnitzler's *Das Weite Land*, Nestroy's *Einen Jux Will Er Sich Machen*, and Molnar's *Play at the Castle*.

Tango (1966)

On 25 May 1966, the Royal Shakespeare Company's production of *Tango* opened at the Aldwych Theatre. In the program Stoppard is acknowledged, but merely. He had not yet achieved sufficient recognition to merit even a comment. It was later in this same year that *Rosencrantz and Guildenstern Are Dead* received its enthusiastic review from Ronald Bryden.

Like Stoppard, *Tango's* author, Polish Slawomir Mrozek, began as a journalist. His collections of humorous and satirical short stories and one of cartoons preceded his short plays, some of which were staged in Poland and later produced on BBC Television. *Tango* is his first full-length play and had been successfully produced in Poland, Yugoslavia, and Germany.

An allegorical lampoon of its times, the play was described by the *Times* critic as "a new variation on the battle of the generations."[2] Arthur, representing the young generation and finding it impossible to return to the ways of the past, "sets himself up over the family as a Superman; but he is too feeble for the role and is ousted and killed by his mother's lover—a working-class tough who concludes the play by dancing a tango" with Eugene, Arthur's grand-uncle. Eddie, the tough, symbolizes naked power, which eventually allies itself with "the old forces of social tradition,"[3] represented by Eugene.

Tango is a domestic farce about members of a family who have given up societal traditions and are living in an anarchic state in a cluttered atticlike home furnished with outlandish, bizarre articles. Stomil, the father, is an artist who insists on the freedom to pursue his theatrical experiments. Since for him tragedy is no longer possible and even farce is boring, the only mode of theater left is experiment. Liberal in his attitudes and rational in his method, he is unperturbed by the affair between his wife, Eleanora, and the uncouth Eddie under his own roof. In addition, there are the grandmother, Eugenia, who spends some of her time in a coffin, and her brother, Eugene, who at one point is imprisoned in a cage by young Arthur, who decides to put some order into the chaotic domestic structure.

Arthur, the son of Eleanora and Stomil, attempts to "create a system in which rebellion will be joined with order and nothingness with existence," for, he argues, "if nothing exists and even rebellion is impossible, what is it that can be created out of nothing and given reality?"[4] His rebellion takes the form of reviving traditions.

His modus operandi is to wed his cousin, Ala, who emerges at one point in the play from under the bedcovers. Enlisting the aid of his traditionalist Uncle Eugene, Arthur organizes a conventional wedding. All dress appropriately, with Eddie resuming the domestic role of butler, in place of the lover and card-player roles formerly enjoyed by him. Complications occur, however, when Arthur learns that his bride-to-be and Eddie had enjoyed sexual relations that very morning. So, Arthur's plans to create a new order, which included the murder of Eugene by Eddie, are disrupted. At the end of the play, it is Arthur who is killed by Eddie and Eugene who dances the tango with Eddie, literally and metaphorically.

Mrozek's drama employs themes and techniques that have come to be associated with Stoppard's plays. There are, first of all, the many debates about revolutions that leave anarchy in their wake. From anarchy, Arthur, a Boot-like character, attempts to create a new order out of the old, but fails.

As in many of Stoppard's plays, Mrozek's characters play assorted games. A card game opens the play; the father's experiments are games; Eleanora and Eddie play their games; the ultimate game of marriage planned by Arthur is a way of organizing the chaos around him; and finally, the tango, a traditional dance referred to early in the play, is executed in the final scene between Eugene and Eddie, symbolic of the bizarre union of the old forms and the new naked power.

The games continue in the famous twists in logic and language that form the basis for the humor and jokes of Stoppard's own plays. At one point Arthur, upset by the bedlam, states: "Grandfather has been dead ten years. And no one has thought of taking away that catafalque. It's unbelievable. It's a wonder they took *Grandfather* away." Eugene replies: "Grandfather was becoming impossible to live with."[5]

In spite of the farcical aspects, the play is just not funny enough, according to the *Times* reviewer. He suggests that the "task of placing jokes in a schematic framework and working to a length beyond his previous range seems to have dulled his [the author's] invention."[6]

The House of Bernarda Alba (1973)

If, as Stomil in *Tango* asserts, tragedy is possible only where rigid social traditions exist, an example of his theory can be seen clearly in Lorca's *The House of Bernarda Alba*. In this tragedy, centuries-old attitudes toward women and sex, determined by the Catholic religion, inevitably create seeds of rebellion. In *Tango* there was nothing to rebel against except the absence of something against which one could rebel. In Lorca's play, the deeply rooted social order provides the basis for a tragic collision between that order and the natural needs of a family of women without men.

The matriarchal family consists of a mother and five daughters who are prisoners of the prevailing conventions. The more repressive the strictures, the more violent the urgent sexual demands against that order become. "We are all cursed by being born" and "Being born a woman is the worst possible punishment"[7] are the women's cries that permeate the play.

When the eldest daughter, forty years old, is entitled to the affection of the local eligible male, it is the hunchback daughter who has a "fire raging between my legs,"[8] and it is the youngest daughter to whom the bachelor is attracted (she later commits suicide).

The *Plays and Players* reviewer found in Stoppard's adaptation "a note of detached, Anglo-Saxon flippancy," with "too much of the pettish Home Counties schoolgirl in Augustias. 'Anyone who doesn't like it can stick it. . . .' " Only Patience Collier (who had played Eugenia in *Tango*, incidentally) achieves the "foreign feel." The powerfully elemental forces at work in Lorca's drama come off more as "token scrapping of the order of playground pique."[9] Perhaps Stoppard may have fallen into what he describes as the "Knightsbridge" trap.

Stoppard has talked about two sources for his "faithful" adaptation: "one is the Penguin, done in the 40's," and the second is "a literal translation from a girl who has been reading Spanish and drama at Bristol University. Her name's Katie Kendall and she's also supplied me with notes and some of her ideas as well."[10]

An example of the way he works from a literal translation can be found in his rendition of a line by Bernarda: "What a poverty I have, not having a flash of lightning between my fingers."[11] Stoppard's version reads: "My God I am poor in means to pay you—I should have the power to strike you dead with my raised finger."[12] His adaptation illustrates his attempt to be natural. Fidelity suffers, however, in the elimination of the lightning imagery. Lorca is a poet in the theater, and his effects depend substantially on the powerful, elemental images without which he is emasculated.

Undiscovered Country (1979)

When asked what motivated him to adapt Schnitzler's play, Stoppard replied: "What it was—while rehearsing *Night and Day* in a church hall in Chelsea, I saw a copy of a literal translation of *Undiscovered Country* on Peter Wood's table. I was just being nosy. They had asked somebody to adapt it, but he pulled out. My interest was partly because Peter Wood would direct it and John Wood would act in it. Once I read the play, I agreed with Peter. It was remarkable, a play completely unknown in England, and worthy to stand with Ibsen and English contemporaries."[13]

Acknowledging himself as "a writer with no German," Stoppard wrote from a literal translation provided by the National Theatre and with the "services of a German linguist, John Harrison."[14] Together they "went through the play line by line, during which process small corrections were made and large amounts of light were shed on the play. . . . After several weeks of splitting hairs with Harrison over alternatives for innumerable words and phrases, the shadings of language and character began to reveal themselves: carving one's way by this method into the living rock is hardly likely to take one around the third dimension, but as the relief becomes bolder so does the translator until there is nothing to do but to begin" (11). Stoppard's version is shorter than the original. Unable to resist the temptation to "add a flick here and there," he says the work is not a translation but rather "a record of what was performed at the National Theatre" (12).

Set in the pleasure-seeking Vienna of 1902, the play is an opulently clinical analysis of the leisure class, whose daily lives are defined by the games they play. Among others, the games consist of climbing, tennis, marital infidelities, and even the traditional duel. Schnitzler, "a Viennese doctor and psychologist admired by his contemporary, Sigmund Freud, was adept as the master at probing the dark side of the psyche and as skillful a remover of manhole lids."[15]

With a cast of more than fifty, Schnitzler paints a detailed picture of the conversational patterns, the behavior, and the cynical attitudes that create the very structure of the play. His view of society has been described as a "landscape that takes its inspiration from the paintings of Gustav Klimt, who was a contemporary of Schnitzler's."[16]

At the center of the play's action are Friederich Hofreiter, a philanderer, and his faithful wife, Genia. When she does not submit to the advances of a would-be lover, he commits suicide. For her marital fidelity Genia is rewarded by reproaches from Friederich. Subsequently she does take a lover, and her affair is the cause for the duel between husband and lover, in which the latter is killed. The play begins with a funeral and ends with a death.

Simple and romantic though the main plot may seem, Schnitzler's complex play is an impressive dissection of an entire society. The individuals and families that revolve in the orbit of the Hofreiters seem only to reinforce and richly embroider the events in the lives of the two leading characters. Details of dress, manners, behavior, attitudes, and, particularly, the insistence on adhering to traditional conduct patterns create a densely woven texture of a Viennese era.

In his review, John Barber points to some of the questions and contradictions inherent in Schnitzler's clinical probing: "How can a man deceive whom he still loves inexpressibly? How can he distinguish between adoration and infatuation? What brings to an end her ironclad devotion?"[17] The answer to these questions is attempted, perhaps, in an important passage in the play, one from which the title derives:

Why I betrayed her? *You* ask *me*? Haven't you ever thought what a strange uncharted country is human behaviour? So many contradictions find room in us—love and deceit . . . loyalty and betrayal . . . worshipping one woman, yet longing for another, or several others. We try to bring order into our lives as best we can; but that very order has something unnatural about it. The natural condition is chaos. Yes, Hofreiter, the soul . . . is an undiscovered country as the poet once said . . . though it could equally well have been the manager of the hotel. (61)

The poet alluded to in the above quotation is obviously Shakespeare and the particular passage that from *Hamlet* in which the young prince in the famous "To be or not to be . . ." soliloquy mentions "the undiscovered country, from whose bourn no traveller returns."[18]

Writing about eighty years prior to Stoppard's adaptation of the play, Schnitzler could hardly have dealt with a more Stoppardian theme. References to the contradictory nature of life, to the chaos of things, and, consequently, to the need for order abound. The probing of the nature of love, betrayals, deceits, and their accompanying contradictions constitutes the subject of Stoppard's own play *The Real Thing* (1982), albeit without the rich social texture that Schnitzler achieves in the brilliant tapestry of his time.

Like the next stage adaptation to be discussed, *Undiscovered Country* is located in Austria (Vienna), which adjoins Stoppard's native Czechoslovakia. The success of *Undiscovered Country* and *On the Razzle* contrasts sharply with the qualified critical reception of the two previous stage adaptations (*Tango* and *The House of Bernarda Alba* with which Stoppard took fewer liberties).

On The Razzle (1981)

The fourth of Stoppard's stage adaptations and the second of Viennese origin, *On the Razzle*, has an impressive theatrical ancestry. In 1835, John Oxenford, drama critic of the *Times* (London) for twenty-five years, wrote a fifty-minute farce, *A Day Well Spent*.

Then in 1842 an actor-manager, Johann Nestroy, having "found a plot like the Oxenford farce . . . set about transforming it to suit the talents of his company. . . ."[19] He titled his play *Einen Jux Will Er Sich Machen*. In 1938, Thornton Wilder adapted the Nestroy farce to a New York setting in *The Merchant of Yonkers*, revising it as *The Matchmaker* after World War II. The next transformation occurred as the musical *Hello, Dolly!* *On the Razzle* is the latest manifestation of the Oxenford plot of *A Day Well Spent*.

Stoppard has said that "the two essentials which this play takes from the original are, firstly, the almost mythic tale of two country mice escaping to town for a day of illicit freedom, adventure, mishap and narrow escapes from discovery; and, secondly, the prime concern to make the tale as comic an entertainment as possible."[20] He further acknowledges a debt "to Neville and Stephen Plaice who prepared a close literal translation . . ." (7).

In a return to the scene of his phenomenally successful *Rosencrantz and Guildenstern Are Dead*, *On the Razzle* was first produced at the Edinburgh Festival. Shortly thereafter, on 18 September 1981, it opened at the Lyttleton Theatre.

The well-known plot involves the escape to the city of two grocer's apprentices for a day on the town or "on the razzle." One of them wishes to have at least one memorable time in his life to remember in his later years. Their boss also happens to be in the city on that day with his fiancée. All kinds of complications pile up, as the pair try to avoid running into their employer. Stoppard, in his version, decided to "go the full hog and make it [a] Scottish fortnight in Vienna,"[21] just as Wilder had made his an escape from Yonkers to Manhattan.

The reviews of the production focused on the changes in the new version and on the linguistic fireworks, which for some critics are and for others are not as striking as in Stoppard's previous adaptations.

Irving Wardle of the *Times* admired "the inspired lunacy that takes
possession of the show once it gets into its stride."[22] He admires
"most of all, the amazing linguistic tangles which, whether spiralling
off into a void or forcing the characters into fresh lunatic actions,
mark out the text as verbally Stoppard's best sustained fireworks to
date."[23] Peter Branscombe of the *Times Literary Supplement* in a mixed
review described Nestroy's language as "brilliantly inventive, precisely rhythmed and modulated, strong in word-play spanning High
German and Viennese dialect,"[24] whereas Stoppard's lacks "the con-
fident command of every nuance of idiom" and is ultimately rootless,
"despite all the effort at localization."[25] And James Fenton sees the
play as "about nothing at all," as contrasted with the strong social
commentary present in the Nestroy play. For him the Scottish jokes
based on clichés and the high proportion of bad puns as opposed to
good-bad puns, are "based on sexual innuendo [and] are extremely
repetitive and at odds with the original."[26]

Rough Crossing (1984)

In *Rough Crossing* Stoppard once more adapts for the stage a central-
eastern European drama, this one previously seen by English audiences in P. G. Wodehouse's *The Play's the Thing.* Having already
adapted Mrozek's *Tango* and plays by Schnitzler and Nestroy in *Undiscovered Country* and *On the Razzle,* he continues the tradition with
Hungarian dramatist Ferenc Molnar's *Play at the Castle,* retitled *Rough
Crossing.* The new title results from a shifting of the play's locale from
the villa in the original to a liner crossing the Atlantic. The popular
boulevard comedy being written in Molnar's drama about two writers
becomes a musical comedy. Jokes and song-and-dance routines by the
writer and composer replace Molnar's "wonderful ear for character as
it reveals itself in colloquial speech."[27] The jokes include "one-liners,
bi-lingual puns, idioms triply fractured by foreigners, mishearings
and mistimings, misreadings and mistypings."[28] A major joke-inven-
tion is the addition of a ship's steward who "preempts the partners'
discussion on the art of exposition by delivering a full account of the
dramatic situation in faultless synopsis-writer's English. As a waiter
he also has an unerring ability to pounce on harmless remarks as an
invitation to have a drink."[29] Stoppard expands Molnar's cast of six
to sixteen, and he adds music by André Previn, who composed the
music for *Every Good Boy Deserves Favour.*

In regard to his adaptations, Stoppard finds it "liberating to be given the plot and characters, because the bit I like doing best is then there to be done." His "particular twitch is to try to make the lines funny."[30] Plot and character are the nuts and bolts he has frequently mentioned, and once given these what remains is the invention of humor. The production of *Rough Crossing* was directed by Peter Wood, with whom Stoppard has worked for twelve years and who directed *Jumpers*, *Travesties*, *Night and Day*, and *The Real Thing*.

Screenplays

Written after successes with many stage, radio, and television dramas, Stoppard's screenplays are yet another polished example of his unique visual and linguistic techniques. They consist of adaptations of the following novels: *The Romantic Englishwoman* by Thomas Wiseman, *Le Meprise* (Stoppard's title, *Despair*) by Vladimir Nabokov, *The Human Factor* by Graham Greene, and *Innocent Blood* by P. D. James. The directors of the films are among the best: Joseph Losey, Rainer Werner Fassbinder, Otto Preminger, and Mike Nichols respectively. At the time of this writing, *Innocent Blood* is unproduced.

The Romantic Englishwoman (1975)

Written in collaboration with the novelist, Wiseman, *The Romantic Englishwoman* is described by Stephen Farber as "a neglected film about modern marriage" that he suspects "will be around long after this season's flashier, more commercial films have been forgotten."[31] Most reviewers commented on the similarity of the film to Pinter's screenplays of *Accident* and *The Servant*, also directed by Losey. What may be of special interest, however, is the similarity of characters, situation, and theme to Stoppard's *The Real Thing*, produced seven years later.

The plot concerns a successful novelist and screenwriter and his wife, who "think they have nothing when they have everything."[32] The bored wife, Elizabeth Fielding, goes off on a holiday to Baden-Baden where she meets a self-styled poet, also an adventurer. After her return to England, he shows up and is invited by the husband, Lewis, to stay with them at their elegant Weybridge home in Surrey. Lewis is writing a film about a bored and liberated Englishwoman, and he, too, is bored with having to write another routine plot that he would like to turn into a thriller. He hopes that his own domestic situation will provide him with material for his script.

The Lewis home in Weybridge is full of mirrors. "The mirrors glitter; the kitchen machinery clatters; the *au pair* pouts; and the central trio bite off their lines, play deviously with hypocrisies and humiliations, and seem slightly aware that they're creations by artifice out of artificiality."[33] The plot finally does indulge in some thrills "with pursuits on the Riviera and a gangland farewell to Helmut Berger's pale adventurer."[34]

Played by Michael Caine and Glenda Jackson, the roles of husband and wife received strong notices from the critics. Their mutual suspicions and fantasies are portrayed convincingly, as in Elizabeth's searching, upon her return, for evidence of Lewis's possible infidelity. (A variation of this action occurs in the first scene of Stoppard's *The Real Thing*.) Lewis, on the other hand, invites the poet-gigolo to visit with the deliberate intention of observing Elizabeth and him for possible signs of an affair. Ambiguities abound in their mutual suspicions and fantasies. Boundaries between illusion and reality become blurred and provide the suspense for this "film of feeling, tact and intelligence."[35] Caine and Jackson are "well cast, for the multiple discontents of Loseyland linger like powerfully reflected images of other films, other mirrors."[36]

In retrospect, this screenplay seems a source of the similar plot, characters, and theme in *The Real Thing*. This later drama is about a similar trio of characters: a dramatist, his bored wives, and their lovers, among whom is a boorish dramatist with some of the same stylistic infelicities as the self-styled poet of Wiseman's work. The similarities extend even to specific scenes; in one the wife returns from a trip to Baden-Baden and in the other from a supposed trip to Switzerland.

Despair (1978)

Adapted from Nabokov's *Le Meprise*, *Despair* was one of the most anticipated films at the Cannes Film Festival in 1978. But reality fell short of expectations, and most of the reviews were mixed, in spite of unanimous praise for Dirk Bogarde's performance as an aging chocolate manufacturer, Spengler, in Germany of the Third Reich.

Spengler is a "double" character, a doppelgänger who "escapes from the jungle of an honourable existence and penetrates the free and beautiful world of madness."[37] Alan Brien describes him as a "divided man in 'a crisis of identity' who tries to escape his fate by becoming his own twin."[38] But there is a real double for the chocolate manufacturer in the person of a tramp, who provides homosexual overtones to the main character.

At one point Spengler "strips him naked to search for scars, cuts his hair and pares his toe nails, before killing him."[39] The attraction between the two men contrasts sharply with Spengler's "elephantine couplings" with his wife, "a mountainous sausage of a *hausfrau* who looks as if she had been poured into her skin but forgotten to say 'when'. . . ."[40] Eventually the farcical sexual antics of the couple fade away as the emphasis shifts to the identity crisis of Spengler.

Although Phillip Bergson describes Stoppard's script as succulent, Brien finds the usual Stoppardian jokes "unexpectedly tentative, and easily missed, while the plot sprouts all kinds of surreal creepers many of which spend a great deal of screen time and space wandering nowhere."[41] Yet some of the familiar Stoppardian language tricks do appear, such as the one in which the chocolate manufacturer "claims to be writing a book about split-personality, adding under his breath 'two books perhaps?' "[42] And there are the visual spectacles such as "Bogarde visiting the rival chocolate factory where bulbous, edible babies circulate on a conveyer belt giving the Hitler salute; SA troopers ineffectually pelting a shop-window with bricks which bounce off; the picnic outing to The Lakes which turn out to be one small lily-pond from which Volker Spengler emerges, refreshed, and freckled with mud."[43]

As in *The Romantic Englishwomen* and *The Real Thing*, *Despair* includes a phoney artist with whom the wife has an open affair that provides some farcical moments.

The inspired Nabokovian lunacy of the divided character provides Fassbinder with still another vehicle for his criticism of Nazism and the bourgeoisie, and it provides Stoppard with much opportunity to exercise his talent for grotesque and surreal visual effects. Indeed, the total effect of the film, according to Brien, is of "a banquet of sumptuous *hors d'oeuvres* which never adds up to a meal, suggesting that once again his, Fassbinder's, eyes are bigger than our bellies."[44] And another reviewer asks whether "familiarity with an evil, through the glossy medium of the film, does not reduce one's contempt for it. In a lacklustre present the nostalgia for the thirties is understandable. Can we be sure that this new found fascination is only superficial?"[45]

The Human Factor (1979)

"You needn't have stuck so closely to my original."[46] Graham Greene's comment to Stoppard reflects the confidence of the novelist in the dramatist. In fact, Greene stayed away from the filming of his novel and talked with Stoppard on the telephone only for the purpose of exchanging ideas. The filming was done in Greene's home town of Berkhamstead.

With Stoppard's penchant for the detective/mystery element, prevalent throughout his writing, the Greene novel about a mole in the British secret service, a double agent who spies for the U.S.S.R., was a likely project. The exotic touch, again a hallmark of Stoppard, is provided by the inclusion of a black wife from South Africa. It was, in fact, his helping her escape from her native country that involved him (the mole) in espionage work. The spy, Maurice Castle, is portrayed sympathetically by Nicol Williamson, and his black wife by Iman, the famous model, who makes her film debut here. The formidable cast includes Sir John Gielgud, Sir Richard Attenborough, and Robert Morley.

The publicity surrounding the film at times submerged its content, as articles in both London and New York newspapers focused on the financial difficulties Preminger encountered. Backers had withdrawn from the film and lawsuits followed. Publicity also involved the usual arguments between Preminger and his actors. To add to the film's notoriety, a real spy scandal involving Blunt, in the highest reaches of government, broke at about the time the film was being edited.

Interest in the work was spurred by the fact that Greene had known Kim Philby of the famous spy case that also involved Guy Burgess and Donald MacLean. Their acquaintance dated back to a time when the common enemy of England was Germany and the ally of England was the Soviet Union. Divided loyalties and the clash between conscience and country, already dramatized by Stoppard in *Neutral Ground*, create internal and external conflicts that defy resolution. It was two years earlier that Stoppard's television play about similar conflicts between English academicians and a Czech student appeared, *Professional Foul*.

Innocent Blood (unproduced)

In 1981 prior to the production of *On the Razzle* at the Edinburgh Festival, Stoppard journeyed to Hollywood with the script for the filming of the P. D. James novel *Innocent Blood*. Mike Nichols, the director to whom he presented the script, "expressed satisfaction, but I have not heard anything since. I'm waiting to see if it becomes another of the 100 screenplays from which only one film is made."[47] In the spring of 1982, Stoppard indicated a similar skepticism to this writer about the film's production.

P. D. James (maiden name of Mrs. Phyllis Dorothy White) is regarded as a successor to Agatha Christie by virtue of the series of sophisticated detective novels she has written. In *Innocent Blood*, she has turned psychological novelist for the first time, returning at the end of the novel again to a thriller. Her novel made news when it earned her one million dollars in America even before its publication.

The story concerns the search for her parents by an eighteen-year-old adopted woman, Phillipa Rose Palfrey, about to enter Cambridge. Leaving her stepparents, who had provided her with the advantages of an upper-middle-class station, she discovers that her father had died in prison where he was serving time for raping a Girl Guide. Phillipa's real mother, who had murdered her husband's rape victim, is about to be released from prison. The two accept each other, roam the streets, and find work where they can, in order to subsist. Their freedom, however, is illusory, as the past catches up with them in the person of the Girl Guide's father, who stalks them. The bizarre events of the past lead into an even more bizarre present that is a trap for them. With the appearance of the father who seeks revenge, the story, up to now an interesting handling of the psychological effects of events on mother and daughter, turns into a thriller of the kind James is known for.

The stage adaptations and screenplays reflect substantive and stylistic aspects of Stoppard's original dramas. For example, the problems of the characters in *The Romantic Englishwoman* bear marked resemblance to those of *The Real Thing*.

Stoppard's obvious interest in central and eastern European writers such as Mrozek, Nabokov, Schnitzler, Nestroy, and Molnar finds direct expression in his political plays of the 1970's. His adaptation of Nabokov's *Le Meprise* contains the kind of bizarre spectacles in works such as *Lord Malquist and Mr. Moon*, *Jumpers*, and *After Magritte*. More specifically, Stoppard shares with Nabokov the phenomenon of brilliant linguistic inventions by two Slavic writers for whom English is an adopted language. Critics have frequently allied Stoppard and Nabokov in this respect.

Finally, one cannot omit reference to the bizarrely ironic events involving murder, mystery, spies, double agents, inspectors, etc., that are a part of the plot machinery of so many of Stoppard's radio, television, and stage plays. These elements are the basis for Greene's *The Human Factor* and P. D. James's *Innocent Blood*, which Stoppard adapted.

Novel and play adaptations, along with radio, television, and film scripts, form a large portion of Stoppard's writing. They seem not so much mere preparation for his major stage plays (although this is certainly the case with *Another Moon Called Earth*) as they do a continued, sustained activity in writing, whatever dramatic genre or media is involved. Writing for radio, television, and film has come into its own and is beginning to share equality with stage dramas, particularly in published form.

Chapter Fifteen
The Real Thing

With marital infidelities as a minor theme in a number of his plays, Stoppard finally dramatizes them as the main subject of a bittersweet comedy, *The Real Thing* (1982). Having written his major stage dramas about brilliantly debated ideas on existential philosophy, moral philosophy, art, and journalistic morality, he now debates for the first time the nature of love. What is the real thing?

Although the subject of love is debated, what makes this witty Shavian comedy distinctive is that the intellectual debates do not constitute its main thrust. They are only a part of a complex pattern of constantly shifting personal relationships made perfectly credible for the first time in a Stoppard play. Repeatedly charged with lack of emotional force in his characters, Stoppard has put to rest doubt about his ability to create full-dimensional human characters. He dares, even, to assign the emotional changes in the play to the leading male character and their verbal articulation to the leading female character. Henry, a word-wizard when writing a play or discussing the importance of language, by his own confession is unable to "write love"; neither can he verbalize it in his private life. So the play is about Henry's education in love, an education that involves both pain and joy. His second wife, Annie, is his teacher.

Critical reactions to the play ran the gamut, from Michael Billington's view that the play with its "unequivocal statement about the joyousness of shared passion" is "that rare thing in the West End . . . : an intelligent play about love"[1] to Irving Wardle's verdict that the self-laceration in the play produces a cumulative effect of "cleverness with its back to the wall."[2] Wardle found the performance, especially between the two central characters, "full of mischief, erotic hunger, and human generosity, and . . . did not believe a word of it."[3] To Frank Rich, "Mr. Stoppard's old and new obsessions fight to a fitfully engaging draw. *The Real Thing* feels transitional and tentative; its sincere feelings and potentially dazzling theatrical devices buckle out of shape as the author veers between fresh territory and familiar ground."[4] In his review of the New York production, however, Rich is kinder. He attributes the change to Mike Nichols's new staging and the tightening of the script since the London production.

The sea change is, indeed, noticeable. When the play opened in New York on 5 January 1984, having previewed first in Boston and then for a time in New York, the reception was almost unanimously favorable. With Stoppard's rehearsal rewriting and Mike Nichols's direction, it seemed a different play. What was ironically humorous in the original London version was transformed in New York into razor-sharp lines that at times seemed to border on gags. The initially puzzled reactions of the London audience changed in New York to laughter that flowed effortlessly throughout the evening. Even with changes, the lines contain intelligence and wit that are rare on the modern stage. Like Irving Wardle earlier, John Simon—the bête noir of stage critics—was entertained, although unconvinced.

Henry, a dramatist, and Charlotte, an actress playing the lead in his new play, *House of Cards*, are married and the parents of a precocious seventeen-year-old daughter, Debbie. Another married couple consists of Max, who plays opposite Charlotte in Henry's play, and Annie, an actress and an activist in social causes. This quartet of main characters undergoes a change of marital partners in a situational variation of Noel Coward's *Private Lives* and Edward Albee's *Who's Afraid of Virginia Woolf?*

In the very first scene, Stoppard lays his first ambush for the audience. As Charlotte and Max converse in Pinter-like banalities about her trip to Switzerland, from which she has just returned, the exchanges ripen into acid hostilities, as Max reveals that he discovered her passport in her recipe drawer. Her lying about a supposed business trip for her employer, Sotheby's, establishes the basis for much of the play's actions, in which truths and lies vie with each other to cause havoc in the emotional life of the main character. In an ironic, minimalist statement, Max comments that their marriage might still be ideal, except for this small incident—the discovery of a lie.

Stoppard's joke on the audience is that it is not clear until the following scene that this first scene is an on-stage performance of an act from Henry's *House of Cards*. As a temporary ambush for the audience, the joke becomes serious as it is continued offstage in the real lives of the characters. This kind of confusion or audience ambush is but another variation of the one in *Night and Day*, in which the deliberate confusion between Ruth's spoken and unspoken thoughts was carefully calculated for effect.

On the day after the performance, Charlotte and Henry discuss the play, particularly Charlotte's dissatisfaction with her role as written. Since in the inner play she carries on an affair with an imaginary lover, she feels a victim of Henry's fantasy. As victim, she argues, she loses the interest of the audience. In the increasingly abrasive dialogue between husband and wife, one senses deeper dissatisfactions than those with her role.

When Max arrives, having been invited by Henry, Charlotte is not hospitable and is even less so when Annie appears with her bag of vegetables rather than the usual congratulatory flowers. Hostilities deepen in the rancorous banter, reminiscent more of Edward Albee than of Noel Coward. Henry, especially, takes advantage of the good nature of Max and turns on him in much the same way George attacks Nick in the Albee play. While Charlotte and Max prepare a dip in the kitchen, Henry and Annie covertly kiss. It becomes obvious that Charlotte is aware of the affair between her husband and Annie, while Max remains naively unsuspicious. Not until some time later, when Max confronts Annie with Henry's hankerchief, found in their car, does he find out from Annie that she loves Henry. Shocked and desperate, Max embraces Annie as she endures his embrace with a blank face.

The next scene opens with what seems a continuation of the previous one, except that the partners are now Annie and Henry. Articulate and charming, she halts amorous attempts by Henry, wishing rather to have a serious talk. She mentions Max's unhappiness and her curiosity about what she thought was their (her and Henry's) sexless night. Then picking up a script, she rehearses with Henry the seduction scene from Strindberg's *Miss Julie*, beginning yet another play-within-a-play metaphor for her current relationship with Henry. *Miss Julie*, frequently described as one long seduction scene, is an apt metaphor, as Annie works her seduction on Henry professionally as well as personally. She becomes involved with an activist-dramatist who wishes to further his causes by means of a television play. Only with the help of Henry would the production be possible, and Annie cajoles Henry into helping rewrite the play.

Thus the interweaving of Henry's *House of Cards*, Strindberg's *Miss Julie* and Stoppard's *The Real Thing* begins a drama of mirrors in which art and life reflect and refract each other. Personal and professional relationships mirror each other in a succession of cryptic and sometimes deliberately confusing scenes.

The subject of love fuses with the subject of art, as Henry confesses his inability to write love, contending that "loving and being loved is unliterary."[5] To write about love, he asserts, is to express happiness in banality and lust. It makes him nervous. Their reading from *Miss Julie* concludes with "tell me I'm a Don Juan," read by Henry, who then abruptly inserts his own line, "tell me I'm a ram." Pushing away from his embrace, Annie reminds him that he becomes moody whenever he is seduced from his work, as in his seduction by "Miranda Jessop on the television" (41–42). Her fantasy example recalls Henry's providing Charlotte with only a phantom lover in *House of Cards*. Henry's fantasy and Annie's reality collide.

Underneath the meandering conversation, unspoken concerns rise to the surface, as Annie demonstrates how subtext should be read. Henry reads his lines uncomfortably. Skirting the real issue, their conversation veers from topic to topic: Annie's charity work, her prison visiting, and, finally, to the dramatist Brodie, whose social causes and loutish playwriting Henry detests. Differences sharpen as Annie, having earlier commented that their honeymoon is over, now accuses Henry of not loving her the way she loves him. "I'm just a relief after Charlotte, and a novelty" (44). As with Charlotte, Henry has failed Annie. To both Charlotte and Annie, he seems at least partly phantom, like the lover in *House of Cards*.

Annie's professional seduction of Henry is realized two years later (act 2), as he finds himself rewriting Brodie's play at her request. As Charlotte used to do, Annie chides Henry about his taste for popular music—Neil Sedaka, the Supremes, Brenda Lee. But the small talk is only a disguise for the real thing, which is Henry's contempt for Brodie as a playwright and his jealousy of Brodie as a personal rival. When Annie insists that Brodie has something to say and that even a bad play is justified by its message, personal and professional antagonisms in Henry fuse. Arguing that "there's something scary about stupidity made coherent" (52), he picks up an old cricket bat, using it as a demonstration of his theory of writing, much as George Moore in *Jumpers* used a hare, tortoise, and bow and arrow to explain his philosophy. Henry's theories of art, unlike Brodie's and very much like those of Joyce in *Travesties*, include the autonomous nature of art:

This thing here, which looks like a wooden club, is actually several pieces of particular wood cunningly put together in a certain way so that the whole thing is sprung, like a dance floor. It's for hitting cricket balls with. If you get it right, the cricket ball will travel two hundred yards in four seconds, and all you've done is give it a knock like knocking the top off a bottle of stout, and it makes a noise like a trout taking a fly. . . . What we're trying to do is to write cricket bats, so that when we throw up an idea and give it a knock, it might . . . *travel*. . . . Now what we've got here [picking up the script] is a lump of wood of roughly the same shape trying to be a cricket bat, and if you hit a ball with it, the ball will travel about ten feet and you will drop the bat and dance about shouting "Ouch!" with your hands stuck into your armpits. (53)

For Henry, style is all, and whether or not a play "will travel" depends on style, not message, particularly the kind of revolutionary message Brodie's plays contain. The difference between Henry's dramatic "cricket bat" and Brodie's "lump of wood" is a sharp one.

Expressionless, Annie watches him hop about with his hands in his armpits and then tries to persuade him to cut and shape Brodie's play. Frustrated, he complains that "if Charlotte had made it legal with that architect she's shacked up with, I'd be writing the real stuff" (55). Ironically, it is an architect who is the central male character in *House of Cards* and it is an architect who is Charlotte's current lover. Life and art wittily weave their way through the current argument between Annie and Henry.

We next see Annie in a first-class compartment on a train to Glasgow, where Billy, her leading man in *'Tis a Pity She's a Whore*, a seventeenth-century play by John Ford, pops in with the very lines Annie and Henry in the previous scene had been reading from Brodie's play. Gently chiding Annie for traveling first class while espousing Brodie's social causes, Billy is met with her defense: "it's a cultural thing; it's not *classes* or *system*. . . . There's nothing really *there*—it's just the way you see it. Your perception" (58). Her arguments, like those of Dotty in *Jumpers*, are drawn from feelings and intuition. Annie might well be a vindication of what Professor Ayer in his article on *Jumpers* has called the possibility of "love among the logical positivists." Her need, whether a seat on the train or a liaison with Brodie or Billy, must be met.

As Henry had earlier agreed to help Brodie with his play, for Annie's sake, so Billy agrees to perform in that play so long as Annie plays opposite him. Although acquiescing with Henry's verdict that the play is rubbish, Billy knows that Brodie too is right. For Henry's intellectual argument "sounds all right, but you know it's rubbish" (59). Annie reprimands Billy for getting "snotty" and lapses into lines from *'Tis a Pity She's a Whore*, and the two recite a scene from that play. The adultery theme is intensified even in this brief encounter on a train, as their mutual attraction is obvious.

The refraction of life by art continues in the next scene as in her living room Charlotte discusses with Henry the Anabella role she had played earlier in her career, the same one Annie plays now. Henry finds out about Charlotte's affair with the man who had played Giovanni to her Anabella. Henry's suspicions about Annie in a similar liaison are evident. In a quick scene shift to Glasgow, we see Annie and Billy, wearing rehearsal clothes, kissing and embracing. Stoppard's script reads that Annie returns the play kisses in earnest.

Of all the scenes in the play, that which has drawn unanimous critical approval in both London and New York is the one in which Henry has a fatherly chat with his precocious daughter, Debbie. Sexually liberated at seventeen, she confides to him her initial and subsequent affairs, just as Charlotte had done earlier. Indeed, Debbie reminds Henry of Annie as she (Debbie) defines free love as being free of propaganda. As Henry ruminates the nature of love, particularly the difference between loving and making love, he comments about the aftermath, the pain that is left when it is gone. Debbie perceptively picks up the subtext in his comments. "Annie got someone else, then?" she asks. Told not to worry, she admonishes him: "Don't you. Exclusive rights isn't love, it's colonization" (69). This scene with his daughter contains the hard truth that Henry's emotional education must include. The scene serves as a preparation for Annie's arrival from Glasgow.

Henry questions Annie as he had questioned Charlotte earlier. In telling, more than explaining, her liaison with Billy, Annie insists that Henry will have to find a part of himself where she is not important, or he won't be worth loving. His education about love, begun earlier by Charlotte, continued by Debbie, is completed by Annie in the remaining scenes. But before the final, climactic scene there is yet another play-within-a-play encounter between Billy and Annie on the Glasgow train. As they rehearse lines from Brodie's play about the fascist tendencies in the country, the easy rhythm with which their rehearsal and their intimacy flow is obvious.

In one final ambush for the audience, much like that in scene 1, the voices of Annie and Billy are heard, and the audience realizes that a video machine is playing a cassette of Brodie's drama. For the first time Brodie appears. He, Annie, and Henry are previewing the television production. The passage after drinks and small talk is parallel to scene 2 in which the *House of Cards* is discussed by the quartet of main characters. Here Brodie's play is the topic, and, as in the earlier scene, the remarks grow acrimonious. Henry goes after Brodie for his manners, as he had gone after Max earlier. Brodie then jealously attacks Annie about her relationship with Billy, asking if he (Billy) is a "pansy" and if Annie is any different in her personal life from the role she plays in the drama. Insulted, Annie smashes a bowl of dip in his face. Brodie leaves.

Much the wiser, Henry responds calmly to the quarrel between Annie and Brodie: "You should have told me. About Brodie. That one I would have known how to write" (84).

The real thing, Henry learns, is that with the often contradictory joys and pains of marital relationships, it is only by understanding and respecting Annie's needs that he can hold on. Annie has made it clear that Billy holds some attraction for her. She does not change, but Henry must.

The play is Stoppard's second "Priestley" play—about a man, wife, and child. The emotional problems are confronted as they are not in *Night and Day*. The many mirrors refract the images of Henry as a lover, husband, father, and writer in an interestingly contemporary family. Emotionally he experiences the complexities of love and need, and literarily he remains snobbishly superior to Brodie. In both respects he finds himself partial victim, a Moon character for whom Pirandellian confusions of illusion and reality are contained within the concentric events. For Stoppard writes about a cuckolded dramatist (writing about a cuckolded architect), who, against his own aesthetic principles, revises a television drama by his personal antagonist, a drama in which his wife appears with an actor to whom she is attracted. Stoppard's problem play about marriage provides no easy solution, except that of increased understanding on the part of Henry. The understanding affects even the dramatist's art as expressed in his comment that he can finally "write love," as Stoppard himself has finally been able to do.

Chapter Sixteen
Conclusion

Two headlines in the *New York Times* on 19 August 1983 might well serve as metaphors for a Stoppardian vision of contemporary reality and as a basis for a Stoppardian dramatic scenario. One reads: "A Condominium of Glass to Be Erected Near U.N." (p. 85). The article describes the superluxury building, a fifty-five story structure with an upper five-story pyramid of multihued glass topped by an upwardly sloping prismatic pyramid as the distinctive signature of its developers. Sheathed in glass, it is intended to complement existing structures, such as the Chrysler, Empire State, and Citicorps buildings. Such a building might have been included in Stoppard's tribute to America's centennial year, 1976, *New-Found-Land*.

On the front page of the same edition, another headline reads: "Houston's Glass Castles Shatter as the Hurricane Sweeps Inland." Even as one glass skyscraper in New York is projected as an image of its age, others like it in Houston are shattered by the force of Hurricane Alicia.

Structures and storms are part of Stoppard's latest play, *The Real Thing*. In that play an architect constructs a model hotel from cards, a model that collapses with the slam of a door. There is also a storm in the form of a miniature Alp in a glass bowl, a gift to the architect from his unfaithful wife who wishes to cover up a clandestine affair. When the architect shakes the bowl, he creates a snowstorm, and the scene ends with a large screen of a snowstorm that envelopes the stage. This initial scene serves as introduction to the real storm to unfold in the life of a dramatist named Henry. In this real storm a marriage collapses, a new one is built, and this one, too, is threatened with collapse.

Stoppard's fictional dramatist, Henry, and Henry's fictional architect, Max, are but the latest variations of assorted architects and their structures in Stoppard's dramas. There are the philosophical, moral, and artistic architects for whom existing buildings topple or crash and who attempt to preserve them or to create something from the ruins. If successful, these characters are the Boots of Stoppard's world, Boots who attempt to reorder the chaos around them; if unsuccessful, they become victims, Moons, in a long-standing Stoppardian tradition, beginning with his early novel, *Lord Malquist and Mr. Moon*. Thus, Clufton Bay Bridge collapses along with Albert's philosophy in *Albert's Bridge*. Similar gymnastic pyramids and philosophical constructions implode in *Jumpers*. Cosmic events such as moon landings, trivialized by quarreling astronauts, instantly demythologize centuries of romantic attitudes in *Another Moon Called Earth* and *Jumpers*. The Churchhillian hero, a man of action, is replaced by the new hero, one who withdraws and creates his own style in response to the chaos around him.

Stoppard's own journey from Czechoslovakia to England, via Singapore and India, at a very early age, reflects an upheaval created by the events of the World War II period. Had these events not occurred, he would have remained Tomas Straussler, perhaps writing under circumstances like those of Vaclav Havel and Pavel Kohout, fellow countrymen and dramatists.

As things stand, however, Stoppard finds himself in a position to espouse human rights causes in his native Czechoslovakia without fear of reprisal. He has done so in numerous articles, plays, and direct participation in political organizations. Distinguishing "between those countries that use censorship and torture as systems of state and those who use it randomly," he seems an anomaly to his more liberal contemporaries who have been weaned on the new-wave traditions initiated in 1956 by John Osborne's *Look Back in Anger*. As such, he has been the object of well-meaning criticism from such liberal dramatists as David Hare: "Tom is separated from most of the English playwrights in that, as an immigrant to England, he is unreservedly in love with England and he approvingly quotes Kipling: 'In God's lottery, to be an Englishman is to draw first prize.' We have a more jaundiced view of England."[1] Directly affected by the collapse of old political systems in eastern Europe, Stoppard dramatizes his conservative leanings through the use of metaphors or of brilliant debates in which the dismantling process occurs, George Moore in *Jumpers* being the most obvious example. Thus, the toppling of glass condominiums might well join his own metaphors for his unique vision of modern life.

With his political plays and with *The Real Thing*, he has met, head-on, the criticisms that have haunted the productions of his plays: that he lacks social conscience and that his characters lack credible human dimensions. What remains for Stoppard to realize, perhaps, is the convincing characterization of credible characters who may happen to be liberal and committed. Perhaps Annie in *The Real Thing* most closely approximates this reality.

In regard to dramatic style and structure, Stoppard's last two plays, if they can be seen as indicators, tone down both the flashy mind projections (Stoppard's own term) and the skyrocketing language that created the sensational receptions of earlier plays. The reversion to more naturalistic language, experimented with in *Night and Day*, has been perfected in *The Real Thing*. Henry is in control of his ideas and language rather than losing himself in them, as did earlier characters, such as Rosencrantz, Guildenstern, and George Moore. Henry is, indeed, Henry Boot. What is gained in the toning down of ideas and language, however, is accompanied by the loss of vivid linguistic colors, especially for audiences who have developed expectations of poetic theatricality, displayed so consummately in *Travesties*.

The appropriation of plots from other dramatists seems to be undergoing a change as well, in both *Night and Day* and *The Real Thing*. Waugh's *Scoop* is merely an influence in the former; in the latter, although scenes from Strindberg and Ford are used, they are woven as important parts of the actions in Stoppard's original plot. They work realistically and aesthetically, as rehearsals for roles Annie plays and as mirrors for problems in real life.

In midcareer, Stoppard's directions seem to be changing. Nowhere, even in London, is the change as noticeable as in the New York production of *The Real Thing*. If the change does not tax the intellectual and linguistic acumen or the literary familiarity of the elitist audience, neither does it condescend to the popular commercial mentality.

As an Englishman more English than the English, Stoppard's achievements have allied him with the traditions of Shaw and Wilde. Like them he has shattered some dramatic molds. Not yet fifty, he inevitably invites anticipation of a next play and speculation about future directions. Among the uncertainties of writing about a dramatist still in full vigor, however, resides one certainty, that whatever new directions appear, they will not bore.

Notes and References

Preface

    1. Robert Brustein, "Waiting for Hamlet," in *The Third Theatre* (New York, 1969), 148.
    2. Martin Gottfried, review of *Rosencrantz and Guildenstern Are Dead, Women's Wear Daily*, 17 October 1967.
    3. Irving Wardle, "Cleverness With Its Back to the Wall," *Times* (London), 18 November 1982.
    4. Kenneth Tynan, "Withdrawing with Style from the Chaos," in *Show People: Profiles in Entertainment* (New York, 1979), 64.
    5. Ibid., 64–65.
    6. Frank Rich, "Love Lost and Found," *New York Times*, 6 January 1984, sec. C, p. 3.
    7. Ibid.

Chapter One

    1. *Rosencrantz and Guildenstern Are Dead* (New York, 1967), 39; hereafter cited in text.
    2. "Ambushes for the Audience: Towards a High Comedy of Ideas," Editorial interview with Tom Stoppard, *Theatre Quarterly*, May–July 1974, 3.
    3. Ibid., 5.
    4. Tynan, "Withdrawing," 46–47.

Chapter Two

    1. John Barber, *Daily Telegraph*, 1 December 1977.
    2. Tom Stoppard, "Playwrights and Professors," *Times Literary Supplement*, 13 October 1973, 1219.
    3. "Something to Declare," *Sunday Times* (London), 25 February 1968, 47.
    4. "Ambushes for the Audience," 6–7.
    5. Frances Hill, "Quarter-Laughing Assurance," *Times Educational Supplement* (London), 9 February 1973, 23.
    6. "Something to Declare," 47.
    7. Mel Gussow,"The Real Tom Stoppard," *New York Times Magazine*, 1 January 1984, 20.

Chapter Three

1. Mark Amory, "The Joke's the Thing," *Sunday Times Magazine* (London), 9 June 1974, 68.
2. Ibid., 71.
3. "Ambushes for the Audience," 5.
4. Ibid.
5. *Enter a Free Man* (New York, 1968), 59; hereafter cited in text.
6. Arthur Miller, *Death of a Salesman* (New York: Viking Press, 1950), 57.
7. Harold Pinter, *The Birthday Party* (New York: Grove Press, 1981), 83.

Chapter Four

1. "Ambushes for the Audience," 5.
2. Ibid.
3. "Reunion," in *Introduction 2: Stories by New Writers* (London, 1964), 123; hereafter cited in text.
4. "Life, Times: Fragments," in *Introduction 2: Stories by New Writers* (London, 1964), 126; hereafter cited in text.

Chapter Five

1. Tynan, "Withdrawing," 54.
2. Janet Watts, "Tom Stoppard," interview, *Guardian*, 21 March 1973.
3. *Lord Malquist and Mr. Moon* (London, 1966), 159–60; hereafter cited in text.
4. Ronald Hayman, *Tom Stoppard* (London, 1979), 8.

Chapter Six

1. Tynan, "Withdrawing," 74.
2. "Ambushes for the Audience," 6.
3. Ibid.
4. Ibid.
5. *Rosencrantz and Guildenstern Are Dead*, 18; hereafter cited in text.
6. Jan Kott, *Shakespeare Our Contemporary* (London: Methuen, 1970), 108–9.
7. Luigi Pirandello, *Six Characters in Search of an Author,* in *Masterpieces of Modern Drama*, eds. Haskell M. Block and Robert Shedd (New York: Random House, 1962), 519.
8. Ibid., 526–27.
9. Clive Barnes, review of *Rosencrantz and Guildenstern Are Dead, New York Times*, 17 October 1967.

10. Martin Gottfried, *Women's Wear Daily*, 17 October 1967.

11. C. W. E. Bigsby, *Tom Stoppard* (London, 1979), 16.

Chapter Seven

1. *New York Times,* 5 July 1983,1.

2. A. J. Ayer, "Love among the Logical Positivists," *Sunday Times* (London), 9 April 1972, 16.

3. *Jumpers* (New York, 1972), 28; hereafter cited in text.

4. Tynan, "Withdrawing," 90–91.

5. Ibid., 93.

6. Ibid., 102.

7. Ayer, "Love Among," 16.

8. Clive Barnes, review of *Jumpers, New York Times*, 23 April 1974.

9. Edwin Wilson, "Stoppard's Gem in a Distracting Set," *Wall Street Journal*, 11 March 1974.

10. Timothy Foote, "Crime and Panachement," *Time*, 11 March 1974.

11. Barnes, review of *Jumpers*.

Chapter Eight

1. Michael Billington, cover of *Travesties* (New York: Grove Press, 1977).

2. *Travesties,* 35; hereafter cited in text.

3. Felicia Londré, *Tom Stoppard* (New York, 1981), 72.

4. Ibid., 168.

5. Ibid., 73.

6. Clive Barnes, *New York Times*, 31 October 1975.

7. T. E. Kalem, "Dance of Words," *Time*, 10 November 1975.

8. Richard Ellmann, "The Zealots of Zurich," *Times Literary Supplement* (London), 12 July 1974, 744.

Chapter Nine

1. (Marc), "A Play for Paul," *Sunday Times* (London), 29 October 1978, 32b.

2. Hayman, *Tom Stoppard*, 139.

3. Ibid., 140.

4. *Night and Day* (New York, 1979), 48; hereafter cited in text.

5. Benedict Nightingale, "Have Pinter and Stoppard Turned to Naturalism?," *New York Times*, 3 December 1978, sec. D, 4.

6. Ibid.

7. Bigsby, *Tom Stoppard*, 36.

8. (Marc), "A Play for Paul," 32.

Chapter Ten

1. "Ambushes for the Audience," 8.
2. Ibid., 7.
3. Tynan, "Withdrawing," 67.
4. "Ambushes for the Audience," 17.
5. Ibid.
6. *After Magritte* (London, 1971), 96–97.
7. Tynan, "Withdrawing,"45.
8. Playbill of *Dirty Linen* and *New-Found-Land*, Arts Theatre, 1976.
9. *"Dirty Linen"* and *"New-Found-Land"* (New York: 1977), 65; hereafter cited in text.

Chapter Eleven

1. "But for the Middle Classes," *Times Literary Supplement* (London), 3 June 1977, 677.
2. "Ambushes for the Audience," 13.
3. Ibid., 12.
4. Ibid., 13.
5. Mel Gussow, "Stoppard's Intellectual Cartwheels Now with Music," *New York Times*, 29 July 1979, sec. D, 22.
6. Ibid.
7. Irving Wardle, *Times* (London), 2 July 1977, 7.
8. Ibid.
9. Bernard Levin, *Sunday Times* (London), 3 July 1977, 37.
10. Playbill, *Every Good Boy Deserves Favour*, Mermaid Theatre, 1978.
11. *Every Good Boy Deserves Favour* (New York, 1978), 20; hereafter cited in text.
12. Gussow, "Stoppard's Intellectual Cartwheels," sec. D, 22.
13. Wardle, 7.
14. "Ambushes for the Audience," 12.
15. Ibid.
16. David Pryce-Jones, "Paying the Penalty," *Listener*, 29 September 1977, 419.
17. *Professional Foul* (New York, 1978), 45; hereafter cited in text.
18. Gussow, "The Real Tom Stoppard," 21.
19. *Dogg's Hamlet, Cahoot's Macbeth* (London, 1979), 11; hereafter cited in text.
20. Londré, *Tom Stoppard*, 130.
21. Sean French, "The Art of Faking It," *Sunday Times* (London), 3 January 1984, 55.
22. Peter Kemp, "The Usual Ventriloquist Act," *Times Literary Supplement* (London), 15 June 1984, 667.

23. Michael Church, "Magnificent Shadow-Boxing," *Times* (London), 1 June 1984, 10.

24. Ibid.

Chapter Twelve

1. Hayman, *Tom Stoppard*, 26.
2. Ibid.
3. Ibid., 27.
4. Irving Wardle,"Do Not Miss Stoppard's Radio Play," *Times* (London), 13 July 1967, 8.
5. Ibid.
6. *"Albert's Bridge" and Other Plays* (New York, 1977), 17; hereafter cited in text.
7. Wardle, "Do Not Miss," 8.
8. Bernard Levin, *Sunday Times* (London), 28 November 1976, 38.
9. Hayman, *Tom Stoppard*, 55–56.
10. Ibid., 110.

Chapter Thirteen

1. "I'm Not Keen on Experiments," *New York Times*, 8 March 1970, sec. 2, p. 17.
2. *A Separate Peace,* in *"Albert's Bridge" and Other Plays*, 143; hereafter cited in text.
3. Hayman, *Tom Stoppard*, 79.
4. Ibid., 62.
5. Ibid.
6. Ibid., 63.
7. Ibid., 77.
8. Flora Lewis, "Skeleton from the Closet," *New York Times*, 10 January 1984, sec. A, p. 23.
9. Michael Billington, *Times*, 3 December 1968, 12.
10. "I'm Not Keen," 17.
11. Hayman, *Tom Stoppard*, 82.
12. Gussow, "The Real Tom Stoppard," 22.

Chapter Fourteen

1. Michael Leech, "The Translators: Tom Stoppard," *Plays and Players* 20, no. 7 (April 1973), 38.
2. "Polish Writer's Target in Doubt," *Times* (London), 26 May 1966, 19.
3. Ibid.

4. Slawomir Mrozek, *Tango* (London, 1968), 105.

5. Ibid., 20.

6. "Polish Writers Target in Doubt," 19.

7. W. Stephen Gilbert, review of *The House of Bernarda Alba, Plays and Players,* May 1973, 42.

8. Ibid., 43.

9. Ibid.

10. Leech, "The Translators," 37, 38.

11. Ibid., 37.

12. Ibid.

13. Mel Gussow, "Stoppard's Intellectual Cartwheels," 22.

14. *Undiscovered Country* (London, 1980), 11; hereafter cited in text.

15. John Barber, "Tragi-Comical Study of a Philanderer," *Daily Telegraph,* 21 June 1979, 15.

16. Gussow, "With Stoppard in Schnitzlerland," *New York Times,* 27 February 1981, sec. C, p. 4.

17. Barber, "Tragi-Comical Study," 15.

18. William Shakespeare, *Hamlet,* (act 3, scene 1), in *The Works of Shakespeare* (New York: Oxford University Press, n.d.), 688.

19. James Fenton, "Mr. Stoppard Goes to Town," *Sunday Times* (London), 4 October 1981, 43.

20. *On the Razzle* (London, 1981), 7; hereafter cited in text.

21. Pendennis, *Observer Review,* 30 August 1981, 18.

22. Irving Wardle, *Times* (London), 23 September 1981, 15.

23. Ibid.

24. Peter Branscombe, "The Merchant of Vienna," *Times Literary Supplement* (London), 11 September 1982, 1035.

25. Ibid.

26. Fenton, "Mr. Stoppard," 43.

27. John Peter, "That Sinking Feeling," *Sunday Times* (London), 4 November 1984, 40.

28. Peter Sherwood, "Tricks of the Trade," *Times Literary Supplement* (London), 9 November 1984, 1284.

29. Irving Wardle, "Inventive Abandon," *Times* (London), 31 October 1984, 8.

30. Garry O'Connor, "Two Men on an Ocean Wave," *Sunday Times* (London), 21 October 1984, 39.

31. Stephen Farber, "A Neglected Film About Modern Marriage," *New York Times,* sec. 2, p. 13.

32. Vincent Canby, review of *The Romantic Englishwoman, New York Times,* 27 November 1975, 46.

33. Penelope Houston, review of *The Romantic Englishwoman, Times* (London), 17 October 1975, 11.

34. Ibid.

35. Canby, review, 46.

36. Houston, review, 11.

37. David Robinson, review of *Despair, Times* (London), 26 May 1978, 11.

38. Alan Brien, "A Banquet Without the Main Course," *Sunday Times* (London), 9 July 1978, 37.

39. Ibid.

40. Ibid.

41. Ibid.

42. Ibid.

43. Ibid.

44. Ibid.

45. Phillip Bergson, review of *Despair, Times Educational Supplement* (London), 9 June 1978, 22.

46. David Lewin, "Graham Greene Conjures a Timely Spy Film," *New York Times*, 3 February 1980, sec. D, p. 15.

47. Michael Owen, "Razzle-dazzle Stoppard," *Standard*, 28 August 1981, 24.

Chapter Fifteen

1. Michael Billington, *Guardian*, 17 November 1982.

2. Irving Wardle, "Cleverness With Its Back to the Wall," *Times* (London), 18 November 1982.

3. Ibid.

4. Frank Rich, "Stoppard's *Real Thing* in London," *Times* (London), 23 June 1983, sec. C, p. 15.

5. *The Real Thing* (London, 1982), 41; hereafter cited in text.

6. Ayer, "Love Among," 16.

Chapter Sixteen

1. Gussow, "The Real Tom Stoppard," 21.

Selected Bibliography

PRIMARY SOURCES

1. Published Plays, Novel, and Short Stories

The works of Tom Stoppard are published by Faber and Faber of London and Grove Press of New York, unless otherwise noted.

After Magritte. London, 1971.
"*Albert's Bridge*" and "*If You're Glad I'll Be Frank.*" London, 1969.
"*Albert's Bridge*" and *Other Plays*. New York, 1977. Also includes *If You're Glad I'll Be Frank, Artist Descending a Staircase, Where Are They Now?,* and *A Separate Peace.*
"*Artist Descending a Staircase*" and "*Where Are They Now?*" London, 1973.
"*Dirty Linen*" and "*New-Found-Land.*" London and New York, 1976.
"*The Dog It Was That Died*" and *Other Plays,* London, 1983. Includes *The Dissolution of Dominic Boot, "M" Is for Moon Among Other Things, Another Moon Called Earth, Neutral Ground.*
Dogg's Hamlet, Cahoot's Macbeth. London: Inter-Action Imprint, 1979.
Dogg's Our Pet. In *Ten of the Best British Short Plays*, edited by Ed Berman. London: Inter-Action Imprint, 1979.
Enter a Free Man. London, 1968; New York, 1972.
"*Every Good Boy Deserves Favour*" and "*Professional Foul.*" New York, 1978.
The (15 Minute) Dogg's Troupe Hamlet. London: Samuel French, 1976.
Four Radio Plays. London, 1984. Includes *Artist Descending a Staircase, Where Are They Now?, If You're Glad I'll be Frank,* and *Albert's Bridge.*
Jumpers. New York, 1972.
"*Life, Times: Fragments*" (short story). In *Introduction 2: Stories by New Writers.* London, 1964.
Lord Malquist and Mr. Moon (novel). London: Anthony Blond, 1966; New York: Alfred Knopf, 1968; London: Faber, 1974; New York: Grove, 1978.
Night and Day. London and New York, 1979.
On the Razzle (adaptation of Johann Nestroy's *Einen Jux Will Er Sich Machen*). London, 1981.
The Real Inspector Hound. London, 1968.
"*The Real Inspector Hound*" and "*After Magritte.*" New York, 1975.
The Real Thing. London, 1982.

"Reunion" (short story). In *Introduction 2: Stories by New Writers*. London, 1964.

Rosencrantz and Guildenstern Are Dead. London and New York, 1967.

A Separate Peace. In *Playbill Two*, edited by Alan Durband. London: Hutchinson Educational, 1969.

Squaring the Circle. London, 1984; New York, 1985.

"The Story" (short story). In *Introduction 2: Stories by New Writers*. London, 1964; *Evergreen Review* 56 (July 1968): 53–55.

Tango (adaptation of Slawomir Mrozek's play, translated by Nicholas Bethell). London: Jonathan Cape, 1968.

Travesties. London and New York, 1975.

Undiscovered Country (English version of Arthur Schnitzler's *Das Weite Land*). London, 1980.

2. Articles

"But for the Middle Classes." *Times Literary Supplement* (London), 3 June 1977, 677.

"A Case of Vice Triumphant" (review of *Venice Preserv'd*). *Plays and Players* 14, no. 4 (March 1967): 16–17.

"Dirty Linen in Prague." *New York Times*, 11 February 1977, 27.

"The Face at the Window." *Sunday Times* (London), 27 February 1977, 33.

"I'm Not Keen on Experiments." *New York Times*, 8 March 1970, sec. 2, p. 17.

"Just Impossible" (review of *The Impossible Years*). *Plays and Players* 14, no. 6 (January 1967): 28–29.

"Commentary on *Orghast* by Ted Hughes." *Times Literary Supplement* (London), 1 October 1971, 1174.

"Playwrights and Professors." *Times Literary Supplement* (London), 13 October 1973, 1219.

"The Positive Maybe." *Author* 78 (Spring 1967):17–19.

"Prague: The Story of the Chartists." *New York Review of Books*, 4 August 1977, 11–15.

"Something to Declare." *Sunday Times* (London), 25 February 1968, 47.

"Yes, We Have No Banana." *Guardian*, 10 December 1971, 10.

3. Interviews and Interview-profiles

"Ambushes for the Audience: Towards a High Comedy of Ideas" (editorial interview). *Theatre Quarterly* 4 (May-July 1974): 3–17.

Amory, Mark. "The Joke's the Thing." *Sunday Times Magazine* (London), 9 June 1974, 65–75.

Gale, John. "Writing's My 43rd Priority." *Observer,* 17 December 1967, 4.

Giles, Gordon. "Tom Stoppard." *Transatlantic Review* 29 (Summer 1968): 17–25. Reprinted in *Behind the Scenes*, edited by Joseph McCrindle, 77–87. London: Pitman, 1971.

Gussow, Mel. "The Real Tom Stoppard." *New York Times Magazine,* 1 January 1984, 18–23, 28.

Halton, Kathleen. *Vogue,* 15 October 1967, 112.

Harper, Keith. "The Devious Road to Waterloo." *Guardian,* 7 April 1967, 7.

Hayman, Ronald. "First Interview, 12 June 1974." "Second Interview, 20 August 1976." In *Tom Stoppard.* London: Heinemann, 1977.

Hill, Frances. "Quarter-Laughing Assurance." *Sunday Times Magazine* (London), 9 February 1973, 23.

Leech, Michael. "The Translators: Tom Stoppard—*The House of Bernarda Alba." Plays and Players* 7 (April 1973):37–38.

New Yorker staff interview. *New Yorker,* 4 May 1968, 40.

Norman, Barry. "Tom Stoppard and the Contentment of Insecurity." *Times* (London), 11 November 1972, 11.

O'Connor, Garry. "Two Men on an Ocean Wave." *Sunday Times* (London), 21 October 1984, 39.

Pendennis. "Dialogue with a Driven Man." *Observer Review,* 30 August 1981, 18.

Smith, A. C. H. "Tom Stoppard." *Flourish* (RSC Club News-Sheet), issue 1 (1974).

Sullivan, Dan. "Young British Playwright Here for Rehearsal of *Rosencrantz and Guildenstern Are Dead." New York Times,* 29 August 1967, 27.

Tynan, Kenneth. "The Man in the Moon." *Sunday Times* (London), 15 January 1978, 33–34.

————. "Withdrawing with Style from the Chaos." *New Yorker,* 19 December 1977, 44–111. Revised and reprinted in *Show People: Profiles in Entertainment*, 44–123. New York: Simon and Schuster, 1979.

Watts, Janet. "Tom Stoppard." *Guardian,* 21 March 1973, 10.

SECONDARY SOURCES

1. Books

Bigsby, C. W. E. *Tom Stoppard.* Writers and Their Work Series. London: Longman, 1976, rev. 1979.

Brassell, Tim. *Tom Stoppard: An Assessment.* New York: St. Martin's Press, 1985.

Cahn, Victor L. *Beyond Absurdity: The Plays of Tom Stoppard.* Rutherford, N.J.: Fairleigh Dickinson Press, 1979.

Corballis, Richard. *Stoppard: The Mystery and the Clockwork.* London: Methuen, 1985.

Dean, Joan Fitzpatrick. *Tom Stoppard: Comedy as a Moral Matrix.* Columbia: University of Missouri, 1981.

Hayman, Ronald. *Tom Stoppard.* London: Heinemann, 1977.

Hunter, Jim. *Tom Stoppard's Plays.* New York: Grove Press, 1982.
Londré, Felicia. *Tom Stoppard.* New York: Ungar, 1981.
Whitaker, Thomas. *Tom Stoppard.* New York: Grove Press, 1983.

2. Articles
Apple, R. W. "Stoppard and Pinter Open to Mixed Reviews." *New York Times,* 26 November 1978, 89.
Ayer, A. J. "Love Among the Logical Positivists." *Sunday Times* (London), 9 April 1972, 16.
Babula, William. "The Play-Life Metaphor in Shakespeare and Stoppard." *Modern Drama* 15 (December 1972):279–81.
Barber, John. "Stoppard's Madness Has Method in It." *Daily Telegraph,* 17 July 1979.
———. "Tragi-Comical Study of a Philanderer." *Daily Telegraph,* 21 June 1979, 15.
Barnes, Clive. "Beware of Tom Bearing Gifts." *New York Post,* 4 October 1979.
———. *"Dirty Linen* Sparkles in Wind of Laughter." *New York Times,* 12 January 1977.
———. *"Night and Day* Is Dazzling." *New York Post,* 28 December 1979.
———. "Stoppard's 'Favour' Is a Playgoer's Gift." *New York Post,* 31 July 1979.
———. Review of *Rosencrantz and Guildenstern Are Dead. New York Times,* 17 October 1967.
———. "Stoppard's Murder Play about Philosophy." *New York Times,* 23 April 1974.
———. Review of *Travesties. New York Times,* 31 October 1975.
Beaufort, John. "Stoppard Play at the Met: An Experiment That Works." *Christian Science Monitor,* 3 August 1979.
———. "Tom Stoppard's Blend of Comic Nonsense." *Christian Science Monitor,* 10 October 1979.
———. "Tom Stoppard's Tricky Look at Press Freedom." *Christian Science Monitor,* 29 November 1979.
———. *"Travesties:* Dazzling Skyrocket of a Play." *Christian Science Monitor,* 6 November 1975.
Bennett, Jonathan. "Philosophy and Mr. Stoppard." *Philosophy* 50 (January 1975):5–18.
Bergson, Phillip. Review of *Despair. Times Educational Supplement* (London), 9 June 1978, 22.
———. "The Stars Look Up." *Sunday Times* (London), 28 May 1978, 35.
Berkowitz, Gerald. Review of *Dogg's Hamlet, Cahoot's Macbeth. Theatre Journal* 39, no. 1 (March 1977):111–12.
Berlin, Normand. *"Rosencrantz and Guildenstern Are Dead:* Theater of Criticism." *Modern Drama* 16 (December 1973):269–77.

Billington, Michael. Review of *Neutral Ground*. *Times* (London), 3 December 1968, 12.

———. Review of *The Real Thing*. *Guardian*, 17 November 1982.

———. Review of *The Real Thing*, *Guardian*, 28 November 1982, 21.

Branscombe, Peter. "The Merchant of Vienna." *Times Literary Supplement* (London), 11 September 1982, 1035.

Brien, Alan. "A Banquet without the Main Course" (review of *Despair*). *Sunday Times* (London), 9 July 1978, 37.

Brustein, Robert. "Waiting for Hamlet." In *The Third Theatre*, 148–53. New York: Alfred A. Knopf, 1969.

Buckley, Leonard. "One Pair of Eyes." *Times* (London), 8 July 1972, 11.

Canby, Vincent. Review of *The Romantic Englishwoman*. *New York Times*, 27 November 1975, 46.

Carroll, Peter. "They Have Their Entrances and their Exits." *Teaching of English* 20 (1971):50–60.

Crossley, Brian M. "An Investigation of Stoppard's 'Hound' and 'Foot.' " *Modern Drama* 20 (March 1977):77–86.

Coveney, Michael. Review of *The Real Thing*. *Financial Times*, 18 November 1982, 17.

Daniell, D. J. "Forward with Stoppard." *Theatre News* (May 1979):20–21.

Durham, Weldon B. "Symbolic Action in Tom Stoppard's *Jumpers*." *Theatre Journal* 32, no. 2 (May 1980):169–78.

Egan, Robert. "A Thin Beam of Light: The Purpose of Playing in *Rosencrantz and Guildenstern Are Dead*." *Theatre Journal* 31, no. 1 (March 1979):59–69.

Ellmann, Richard. "The Zealots of Zurich." *Times Literary Supplement* (London), 12 July 1974, 744.

Ensor, Patrick. "An Actor at the Sheepdog Trials." *Guardian*, 12 November 1982.

"An Ex-Pharmacologist is Archbishop of York." *New York Times*, 5 July 1983, sec. A, p. 6.

Farber, Stephen. "A Neglected Film About Modern Marriage." *New York Times*, 18 January 1976, sec. 2, p. 13.

Fenton, James. "Mr. Stoppard Goes to Town." *Sunday Times* (London), 14 October 1981, 43.

———. "The Real Life of Plays and Players" (review of *The Real Thing*). *Sunday Times* (London), 21 November 1982, 42.

Foote, Timothy. "Crime and Panachement" (review of *Jumpers*). *Time*, 11 March 1974.

Gabbard, Lucina P. "Stoppard's *Jumpers*: A Mystery Play." *Modern Drama* 20 (March 1977):87–95.

Giancaris, C. G. "Absurdism Altered: *Rosencrantz and Guildenstern Are Dead*." *Drama Survey* 7 (Winter 1968–69):52–58.

Gilbert, Stephen W. Review of *The House of Bernarda Alba*. *Plays and Players* 20, no. 8 (May 1973):42–43.

Gitzen, Julian. "Tom Stoppard: Chaos in Perspective." *Southern Humanities Review* 10 (1976):143–52.

Goddard, Donald. "The Unmysterious P. D. James." *New York Times*, 27 April 1980, sec. 7, p. 28.

Gottfried, Martin. Review of *After Magritte* and *The Real Inspector Hound*. *Women's Wear Daily*, 24 May 1972.

———. Review of *Jumpers*. *Women's Wear Daily*, 24 April 1974.

———. Review of *Rosencrantz and Guildenstern Are Dead*. *Women's Wear Daily*, 17 October 1967.

———. "Scrubbing *Dirty Linen* Would Help." *New York Post*, 12 January 1977.

———. "Stoppard's *Travesties*: Literary Farce in a Universal Madhouse. *New York Post*, 31 October 1975.

Gussow, Mel. "Bubbling Babel." *New York Times*, 4 October 1979.

———. "Madman's Will." *New York Times*, 1 August 1979.

———. "Schnitzler's Vienna as Told to Stoppard." *New York Times*, 15 July 1979, sec. D, p. 6.

———. "Stoppard Refutes Himself, Endlessly." *New York Times*, 26 April 1974, 36.

———. "Stoppard's Intellectual Cartwheels Now with Music." *New York Times*, 29 July 1979, sec. D, pp. 1, 22.

———. "With Stoppard in Schnitzlerland." *New York Times*, 27 February 1981, sec. C, p. 4.

Harris, Wendell. "Stoppard's *After Magritte*." *Explicator* 34 (January 1976).

Hobson, Harold. "Stoppard in Bloom." *Sunday Times* (London), 16 June 1974, 38.

Houston, Penelope. Review of *The Romantic Englishwoman*. *Times* (London), 17 October 1975, 11.

Howard, Maureen. "Turning the Thriller Inside Out." *New York Times*, 27 April 1980, sec. 7, p. 3.

James, Clive. "Count Zero Splits the Infinite." *Encounter* 45 (November 1975):68–76.

Kalem, T. E. "Dance of Words." *Time*, 10 November 1975.

———. "Spoof Sleuths, Nix Crix." *Time*, 8 May 1972.

———. "Unstoppable Stoppard." *Time*, 24 January 1977.

Kalson, Albert E. Review of *Every Good Boy Deserves Favour*. *Theatre Journal* 29, no. 4 (December 1977): 563.

Kennedy, Andrew K. "Old and New in London Now." *Modern Drama* 11 (February 1969):437–46.

Kerr, Walter. Review of *Night and Day*. *New York Times*, 28 December 1979.

————. "Tom Stoppard Is Too Lazy to Be Funny." *New York Times,* 23 January 1977, sec. 2, p. 3.

Lask, Thomas. "Publishing: Another Aspect of a Mystery Writer." *New York Times,* 8 February 1980, sec. C, p. 27.

Lee, R. H. "The Circle and Its Tangent." *Theoria* 33 (1969):37–43.

Leonard, John. "Tom Stoppard Tries on a 'Knickers Farce.' " *New York Times,* 9 January 1977, sec. 2, p. 1.

Levin, Bernard. Review of *If You're Glad I'll Be Frank. Sunday Times* (London), 28 November 1976, 38.

————. "The Shining Truth of Tom Stoppard" (review of *Every Good Boy Deserves Favour*). *Sunday Times* (London), 18 June 1978, 38.

————. "Stoppard's Political Asylum." *Sunday Times* (London), 3 July 1977, 37.

Levenson, Jill. "Views from a Revolving Door: Tom Stoppard's Career to Date." *Queen's Quarterly* 78 (Fall 1971):431–42.

Lewin, David. "Graham Greene Conjures a Timely Spy Film." *New York Times,* 3 February 1980, sec. D, pp. 1, 15.

Lewsen, Charles. Review of Young Vic revival of *Rosencrantz and Guildenstern Are Dead. Times* (London), 10 April 1973, 9.

————. "Stoppard Companion to *Hamlet.*" *Times* (London), 12 August 1975, 7.

"Marc." "A Play for Paul" (a note on some origins of *Night and Day*). *Sunday Times* (London), 29 October 1978, 32.

Morley, Sheridan. "New Challenge for Non-Stop Stoppard." *Times* (London), 28 June 1977, 8.

Nightingale, Benedict. "Have Pinter and Stoppard Turned to Naturalism?" *New York Times,* 3 December 1978, sec. D, p. 4.

————. "Stoppard Gets Emotional." *New York Times,* 5 December 1982, sec. H, p. 5.

Owen, Michael. "A New Look at Graham Greene's England." *New York Times,* 19 August 1979, sec. D, p. 15.

————. "Razzle Dazzle Stoppard." *Standard,* 28 August 1981, 24.

Peter, John. Review of *Dirty Linen and New-Found-Land. Sunday Times* (London), 18 April 1976, 37.

Powell, Dilys. "Triangular Variations." *Sunday Times* (London), 19 October 1975, 30.

Pryce-Jones, David. "Paying the Penalty" (review of *Professional Foul*). *Listener,* 29 September 1977, 419.

Review of *Tango. Times* (London), 26 May 1966, 19.

Rich, Frank. "Stoppard's *Real Thing* in London." *New York Times,* 23 June 1983, sec. C, p. 15.

Robinson, David. Review of *Despair. Times* (London), 26 May 1978, 11.

Robinson, Gabriele Scott. "Plays Without Plot: The Theatre of Tom Stoppard." *Theatre Journal* 29, no. 1 (March 1977):37–43.

Ryan, Randolph. "Theatre Checklist No. 2: Tom Stoppard." *Theatrefacts* 2 (May-July 1974):3–9.

Schwartzman, Myron. "Wilde About Joyce? Da! But My Art Belongs to Dada!" *James Joyce Quarterly* 13 (1975):122–23.

Shulman, Milton. "The Politicizing of Tom Stoppard." *New York Times,* 23 April, 1978, 3, 37.

Simon, John. "Theater Chronicle." *Hudson Review* 20, no. 4 (Winter 1967–68):664–65.

Taylor, John Russell. "Tom Stoppard." In *The Second Wave: British Drama for the Seventies*, 94–107. London: Methuen; New York: Hill & Wang, 1971.

———. "Tom Stoppard: Structure + Intellect." *Plays and Players* 17 (10 July 1970):16–18, 78.

Wade, David. Review of *Artist Descending a Staircase. Times* (London), 14 November 1972, 12.

———. Review of *Where Are They Now? Times* (London), 18 December 1970, 16.

Wapshot, Nicholas. "I'm Not Maddie Says Mandy." (review of revival of *Dirty Linen and New-Found-Land* featuring Mandy Rice-Davies of Profumo case fame as Miss Gotobed). *Times* (London), 2 May 1981,14.

Wardle, Irving. "A Link Is Cut" (review of revival of *Rosencrantz and Guildenstern Are Dead* at the National Theatre). *Times* (London), 2 July 1970, 7.

———. "Abundance of Bright Ideas" (review of *Every Good Boy Deserves Favour). Times* (London), 2 July 1977, 7.

———. "Cleverness with Its Back to the Wall." *Times* (London), 18 November 1982.

———. "Drama Unearthed from Elsinore's Depths." *Times* (London), 12 April 1967, 8.

———. "Don't Miss Stoppard's Radio Play" (on *Albert's Bridge). Times* (London), 13 July 1967, 8.

———. "High Farce" (review of *Dirty Linen and New-Found-Land). Times* (London), 3 April 1976.

———. "Laughter Machine" (review of *Enter a Free Man). Times* (London), 29 March 1968, 13.

———. "Lunch-Time Stoppard" (review of *After Magritte). Times* (London), 10 April 1970, 16.

———. "Natural Double" (review of *After Magritte* and *The Real Inspector Hound). Times* (London), 8 November 1972, 13.

———. Review of *The House of Bernarda Alba. Times* (London), 23 March 1973, 17.

———. Review of *Dogg's Our Pet. Times* (London), 15 December 1971, 18.

———. Review of *Jumpers. Times* (London), 3 February 1972, 13.

———. Review of *Night and Day. Times* (London), 9 November 1978, 11.

————. Review of *On the Razzle*. *Times* (London), 23 September 1981, 15.
————. Review of *The Real Inspector Hound*. *Times* (London), 18 June 1968, 12.
Watts, Douglas. "More Verbal Tomfoolery by Stoppard" (review of *Dogg's Hamlet, Cahoot's Macbeth*). *Daily News,* 4 October 1979.
Watts, Richard. "A Drama of High Distinction" (review of *Rosencrantz and Guildenstern Are Dead*). *New York Post,* 17 October 1967.
Weightman, John. "A Metaphysical Comedy." *Encounter* (April 1972):44–46.
Wright, Ann. "Tom Stoppard." In *Dictionary of Literary Biography: British Dramatists Since World War II*, edited by Stanley Weintraub, vol. 13, 2, 482–500. Detroit. Bruccoli-Clark, 1982.

Index